inspired by nature: plants

THE BUILDING / BOTANY CONNECTION

Alejandro Bahamón

Patricia Pérez

Alex Campello

W.W. Norton & Company
New York • London

Arquitectura Vegetal: Analogías entre
el Mundo Vegetal y La Arquitectura Contemporánea
Copyright © Parramón Ediciones, S. A., 2006
English Translation Copyright © Parramón Ediciones, S. A., 2008
Published by Parramón Ediciones, S. A., Barcelona, Spain.

For information about permission to reproduce
selections from this book, write to Permissions,
W. W. Norton & Company, Inc.,
500 Fifth Avenue, New York, NY 10110

For information about special discounts for bulk purchases,
please contact W. W. Norton Special Sales at
specialsales@wwnorton.com or 800-233-4830

Library of Congress Cataloging-in-Publication Data

Bahamón, Alejandro.
[Arquitectura vegetal. English]
Inspired by nature : plants :
the building/botany connection / Alejandro Bahamón,
Patricia Pérez, Alex Campello.
p. cm.
Includes index.
ISBN 978-0-393-73251-1 (pbk.)
1. Architecture—Environmental aspects.
2. Plants in architecture. 3. Nature (Aesthetics)
I. Pérez, Patricia. II. Campello, Alex. III. Title.
NA2542.35.B33 2008
720—dc22
                                                    2007030102

W. W. Norton & Company, Inc.,
500 Fifth Avenue
New York, N.Y. 10110
www.wwnorton.com

W. W. Norton & Company Ltd.
Castle House, 75/76 Wells Street
London W1T 3QT

0 9 8 7 6 5 4 3 2 1

INTRODUCTION 4

LIGHT AND SPATIAL ARRANGEMENT 10
Lucky Drops 12   Atelier Tekuto, Masahiro Ikeda
Sharp Centre for Design 22   Alsop Architects
Las Palmas Parasite 30   Korteknie Stuhlmacher Architecten
Fire and Police Station 36   Sauerbruch Hutton Architects
Children's Room 46   Laboratory of Architecture

WATER CONTROL 54
World Birding Center 56   Lake | Flato Architects
New Barcelona Activa Headquarters 62   Roldán + Berengué Arquitectos
Houses in Maasbommel 68   Factor Architecten

TEMPERATURE CONTROL 74
Somis Hay Barn 76   Studio Pali Fekete Architects
Sfera Building 84   Claesson Koivisto Rune
Mill Center for the Arts 92   Pugh + Scarpa, Eskew + Dumez + Ripple

EXTREME CONDITIONS 98
Mountain Bivouac 100   Miha Kajzelj
Turbulence House 108   Steven Holl Architects
Svalbard Research Centre 116   Jarmund/Vigsnæs Architects
ESO Hotel 124   Auer + Weber Architekten + Assoziierte

DEFENSE 132
Dutch Embassy 134   Erick van Egeraat Associated Architects
Magasin 3 142   Block Architecture
Brillare 148   Klein Dytham Architecture

HOMOLOGIES 154
Südwestmetall Offices 156   Allmann Sattler Wappner Architekten
Leaf Chapel 164   Klein Dytham Architecture
Buffon School 172   Edouard François, Duncan Lewis
Billboard Building 178   Klein Dytham Architecture
Cisneros Fontanals Art Foundation 184   Rene Gonzalez

INDEX OF ARCHITECTS 190

Introduction
Patricia Pérez

Beyond intellectual reasoning, the observation of nature and experimentation have long served as tremendously valuable methods in designing architectural forms. From vernacular constructions to the works of eminent architects, natural forms have always been subject to reinterpretations and applied to the realm of architecture. Although the most recognizable analogies tend to be those that evoke particular effects through their morphological and spatial qualities, the main objective of this book is to reveal the analogical similarities that can exist between contemporary architecture and the vegetal kingdom as a result of adaptation processes. In doing so, the diverse formal, structural and physiological attributes proper to the vegetal element will be analyzed on the basis of the relationship between plants and their surrounding space and environment, comparing the most relevant adaptation and survival methods with those reflected through architecture.

The Evolution of Plant Species as a Guarantee of Adaptation

As Charles Darwin demonstrated in his 1859 book *The Origin of Species*, life is a constant struggle for existence endured only by those that best adapt to their environment. Within the plant kingdom, life is organized with a maximum degree of logic and efficiency, and hence, the process of natural selec-

tion impedes the survival of anything that proves inefficient. It is not surprising, then, that nature has created very similar adaptation processes in plants found at great distances from each other, adaptations that allow them to optimize the use of their resources. In adopting this positivistic view, one could assert that there is no better experimental laboratory than the evolution over centuries, nor a better guarantee of efficiency than the adaptability of certain natural forms to their environment. Today, the study and reinterpretation of natural structures serves, once again, as an intelligent tool in enhancing the design of new architectural works. "Originality is to return to the origin." That is how Gaudí summarized his beliefs in a single phrase, understanding "origin" as nature.

Analogies Between the Botanical World and Contemporary Architecture

The most evident paradigm of analogy between both worlds is the tree, as the most common representative of the plant kingdom, and a tall building as its architectural equivalent. The analogy lies in the notable verticality of both elements and in the coinciding existence of subterranean foundations. In popular language, the expression "concrete jungle" is often used to refer to large cities, in which the term for a particular plant formation (jungle: an area of dense vegetation) is accompanied by the term "concrete,"

in allusion to the terrain on which it is located. The exceptional sense of density and verticality lent by the buildings justify use of the word "jungle" in describing the landscape. The analogy becomes even clearer when analyzing the relation tree-column, or rather, trunk-shaft. The stems of plants in general, and more specifically the trunks of trees, tend to be cylindrical-conical, as a result of their tapering width as they grow in height. A column is a vertical and elongated architectural element that serves to support the weight of a structure, while it can also be employed for decorative purposes. Ordinarily, its section is circular, although it often decreases in circumference as it increases in height. Once again, the popular expression "forest of columns," frequently used to describe the Great Mosque of Córdoba or the Basilica Cistern of Istanbul, points to the formal and functional analogical relation between a forest and an aggregation of columns. From a functional point of view, the trunks can be said to sustain the branches in the same way that the columns offer support to the building. These examples rooted in common language, and many more that could be cited, confirm the existence of these analogies or, at the least, the existence of an irrefutable relationship between architectural and vegetal forms.

Immobility, the Struggle for Efficiency and Competition: Principal Conditions Common to Plants and Architecture

The differences that separate these two worlds may seem greater and more abundant than the analogies that bring them together and that serve as a basis for the argument of this book. Buildings are inert structures, formed by diverse constructive elements that occupy meaningful space in which human beings undertake all kinds of activities. Plants, on the other hand, are living beings that emerge, grow, reproduce, and die. Nevertheless, the majority of superior plants and architectural forms share the extremely important peculiarity of constituting fixed, static systems incapable of moving from one place to another in order to satisfy basic needs. Their situation is definitive, and in maintaining this position, develop sophisticated anchoring and structural mechanisms. This static nature is therefore one of the few indisputable conditions that allow for a straightforward comparison between the vegetal and the architectural realm without resorting to abstract or poetic references. The other fundamental condition, and a consequence of the first, is the struggle for efficiency. As prisoners of their emplacement, plants and buildings share the necessity of optimizing the available resources. This translates into an array of similar ways of competing for light and space, of protecting themselves from biotic and abiotic factors, or of obtain-

ing, storing, or discarding the necessary provisions to execute their functions. In sum, the analogy lies in the different forms of adaptation that arise from a static state. Lastly, it is worth mentioning the phenomenon of competition shared by buildings and vegetation. The agglomeration of individual plants as well as that of architectural structures is the most common form of appearance of plants and buildings on earth. Plant communities and cities, villages, and neighborhoods are structures that, much like their individual components, can also be subject to comparison. Urbanism in architecture and plant sociology in ecology are disciplines that, as will be demonstrated here, can offer parallel readings of the different forms of coexistence that occupy the planet. The strategies generated to support certain interactions between individual plants or buildings and the ability to resist environmental modifications are a few of the topics explored in this book. In order to explain the relationships between the different projects that follow and the vegetal adaptations respective to each, a simple yet rigorously scientific text outlines the most relative points of botanical theory. In addition, botanical illustrations graphically exemplify some of the most evident analogies between the architectural and vegetal realm.

The structure of this book is organized into the following chapters:

Light and Spatial Arrangement
Water Control
Temperature Control
Extreme Conditions
Defense
Homologies

May this selection of architectural examples that consciously or unconsciously incorporate vegetal strategies in their design and the general botanical explanations serve as a stimulus for a return to the search for architectural solutions based on the observation of nature in general and of the plant kingdom in particular as the most visible representation of the existing processes, with the aim of creating new sustainable and efficient architectural forms.

| Positive Phototropism | Heliotropism | Canopy Trees |

Light and Spatial Arrangement

Phototrophic plants, which constitute the majority, are those that synthesize their own food via photosynthesis, the process by which light is transformed into chemical energy.

Positive phototropism | This phenomenon, inherent in practically all superior plant organisms, consists of a growth process in which the direction of sunlight is a determining factor that causes plants to grow toward the source of light by turning or twisting. According to this phenomenon, then, a plant is capable of modifying its regular direction of growth when light changes occur in its environment.

Heliotropism | Some plants not only grow toward light, but also have the capacity to move throughout the day, orienting themselves in relation to the rays of sunlight so as to optimize their light intake. One of the best-known examples of this is the case of the sunflower (*Helianthus annus*), characterized by the ability of its leaves and flowers to move during the day and align themselves perpendicular to solar rays. Aside from the forces that elevate it from the ground and push or direct it toward the light, throughout its evolution this plant has had to develop an infinite number of mechanisms in order to compete with other plants for this resource. Altering itself

over time and adjusting its own cycle to that of the sun and other plants is a common adaptation in many plant communities. Nevertheless, here the struggle for light acquires an especially significant role as an effort to emerge from the shadow and into a luminous space.

Trees | As part of this struggle for light, many species, thanks to their longevity, grow exceptionally tall and form leaves specially shaped to capture sunlight. Reaching over 16 feet (5 m) in height and possessing a sturdy trunk that branches out at a relatively high level, these woody plants are generically denominated as trees. Their trunk or main stem, cylindrical in form, apart from conducting the sap and accumulating nutritional reserves if necessary, constitutes the axis of the plant. From a structural standpoint, it is also the principal element of support, in addition to being the driving element of growth that allows these plants to elevate themselves above the rest.

Canopy trees | In tropical rain forests, the abundance of vegetation prevents practically any light from reaching the ground. In the rain forest understory, where the struggle to capture light is fierce, the leaves of most species grow at the

| Epiphytes | Parasites or Semiparasites | Climbing Plants |

same level to avoid creating shade over one another. The *Parkia pendula*, one of the tallest species found within this habitat, develops a canopy-shaped treetop that spreads out over the neighboring trees and defines the characteristic skyline of tropical wet forests.

Epiphytes | Common in tropical rain forests, these organisms grow on the trunk, branches, or leaves of other plants in order to obtain the necessary light without the need for a robust trunk. Its principal problem is precisely a lack of soil, from which plants obtain water and minerals. The sterile leaves of the *Platycerium* fern form a cavity in the bark of the tree in which they live thanks to the accumulation of humus, the plant's source of water nutrients.

Parasites or semiparasites | Although very similar to epiphytes in their use of other plants as support, parasites and semiparasites have no need to perform photosynthesis to obtain food, or do so only partially. Mistletoe (*Viscum album*), for example, is a semiparasitic plant that grows and feeds on trees, forming suckers called haustoria that penetrate and lodge inside the bark of a tree.

Climbing plants | In contrast to epiphytes, which reside in the treetops from the start to ensure the reception of sunlight, these plants are rooted in the ground and survive by spending a minimum amount of energy. Their lack of large trunks allow them to rise quickly above the shade, climbing other plants, walls, or rocks for which they require an efficient anchoring system in order to adhere to the supporting plant. English ivy (*Hedera helix*), for example, possesses a fastening mechanism that consists of extremely slender roots called aerial roots that grow from the stem and cling firmly to the surfaces on which they grow.

Trees

The remarkable singularity in terms of size, form, or situation of many plots in Tokyo's metropolitan area is a consequence of various phenomena that throughout history have come to form one of the most diverse megalopolises on the planet when it comes to architectural typologies. The urban layout of an old city, the traditional Japanese spirit, the successive aftermaths of the 1923 earthquake and World War II, and above all, the economic resurgence during the second half of the twentieth century have created a unique urban environment, home to over 33 million inhabitants. One of its many peculiarities lies in the broad variety of diminutive buildings extraordinarily inserted into the complex urban fabric, designed to make the most of their limited conditions of accessibility and illumination. This construction forms part of a unique typology capable of taking advantage of a plot with such reduced dimensions that its erection would not have even been plausible in any other urban context: 10 feet (3.2 m) wide at the front, 95 feet (29 m) deep and 28 inches (70 cm) wide at the rear. Moreover, the current regulations demanded a setback of 20 inches (50 cm) from the peripheral walls with respect to the adjacent plots. In order to achieve a single- family home that would provide optimum living conditions and resolve the complex determinants of the project, the architects worked closely with the client and builder to explore all technical possibilities.

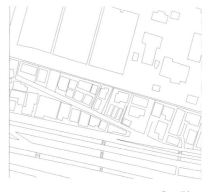

Site Plan

Client
Young couple
Type of Project
Single family home

Location
Tokyo, Japan

Total Surface Area
646 square feet (60 m²)

Year of Completion
2005

Photos ©
Makoto Yoshida

Lucky Drops

Atelier Tekuto, Masahiro Ikeda

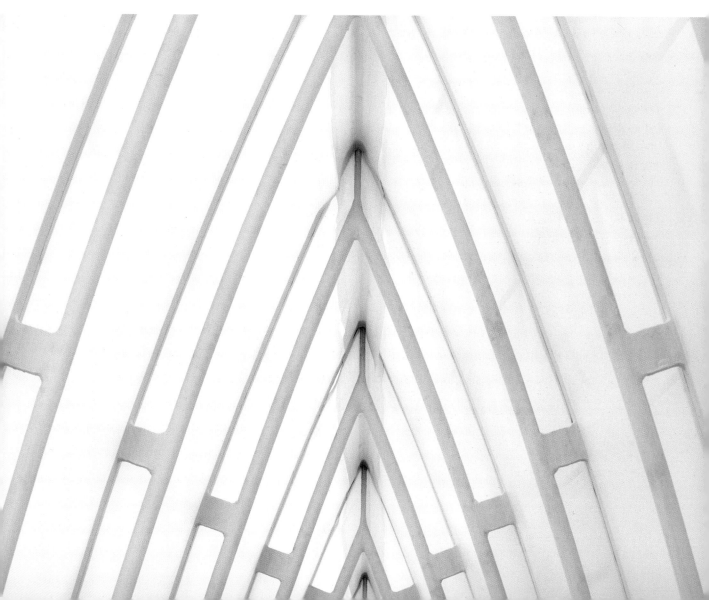

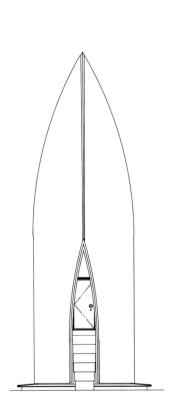

Rear Elevation

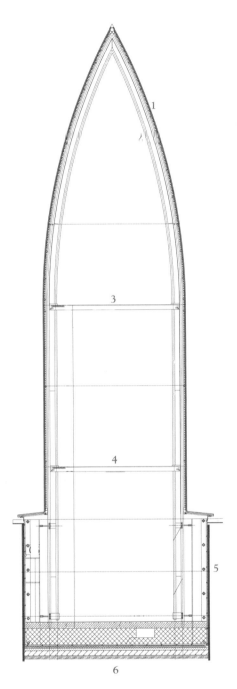

Transverse Section

1- **Waterproof Exterior Wall**
2- **Fireproof Exterior Wall**
3- **Reinforcing Beam**
4- **Entrance Mezzanine**
5- **Steel Panels**
6- **Concrete Slab**

The principal design strategy consisted in creating a building skin that would allow for a naturally illuminated interior and simultaneously preserve the privacy of its occupants. The transverse section of the building exhibits the cladding used to perform these functions: a translucent external skin that permits the passage of natural light into the entire space. Given that any underground construction is exempt from the 20-inch (50-cm) setback regulation, all of the living areas are situated on the basement floor. Instead of the conventional system of ground retention that employs thick walls of reinforced concrete, the architects opted for a panelling system composed of 1/3-inch (8-mm)-thick steel panels coated with an anticorrosive, insulated, and waterproof coating. This method not only reduced the total cost of construction, but also gained an extra 20 inches (50 cm) in interior space.

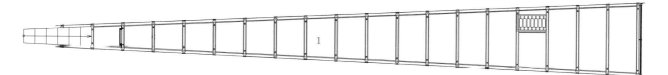

Upper-Level Plan

1- Structural Platform
and Play Area

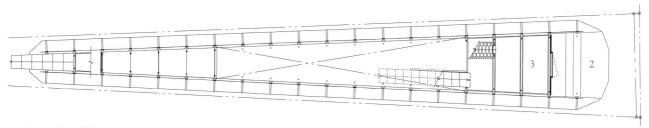

Lower-Level Plan

2- Entrance
3- Vestibule

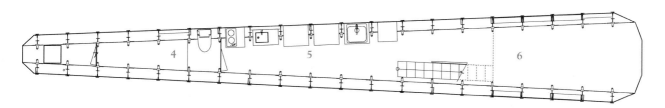

Basement Plan

4- Service
5- Kitchen
6- Living/Sleeping

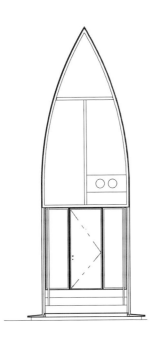

Front Elevation

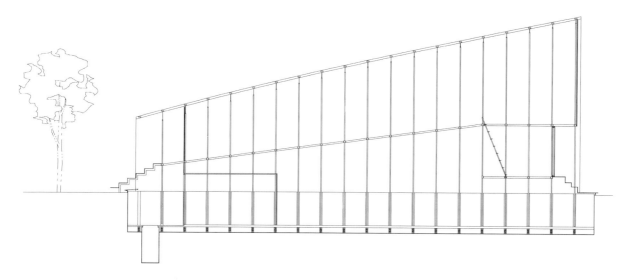

Longitudinal Section

The building adopts the form and size allowed by the plot, creating an interior that tapers from front to rear. The triangular floor plan emphasizes the perspective and creates an effect of depth despite its reduced proportions. In order to structurally reinforce the vault that constitutes the building's skin, an inclined platform runs the length of the interior. This ramp, in addition to its structural function, transforms into a leisure and living area and is composed of perforated metallic sheets that permit light to filter through to the lower space. The name of the project, Lucky Drops, is the translation of a popular Japanese proverb that advocates the virtue of making the most of what could otherwise be put to waste.

Canopy Trees

The Sharp Centre for Design arose out of a governmental initiative, with the objective of expanding and improving the installations for the Ontario College of Art and Design, an internationally renowned institution with a rising number of students. The Centre is located in the western financial district of Toronto, surrounded by university buildings, important arteries and the historic Grange Park, a green lung in the heart of the city. Despite the successive extensions carried out throughout its history, the Centre did not possess the classroom and exhibition space necessary to fulfil the current demands of students. An old open-air parking lot situated south of the main campus building was designated as the plot for the new extension. The team of architects, however, opted for a radical strategy that involved raising a rectangular, two-floor volume, 85 feet (26 m) above the ground. This solution, apart from ensuring a strong visual impact, allowed the integration of the former parking area into the urban fabric, thus generating a connection between the campus and Grange Park. A provocative, unconventional, optimistic, and irreverent building that exhibits the multiple architectural strategies that can be used to produce quality spaces within a densely constructed urban environment.

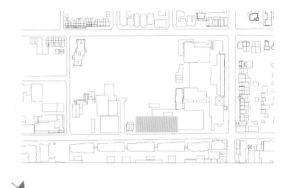

Site Plan

Client
Ontario College of Art and Design

Type of Project
University building

Location
Toronto, Ontario, Canada

Total Surface Area
66,898 square feet (6,215 m²)

Year of Completion
2004

Photos ©
Tom Arban, Richard Johnson

Toronto, Ontario, Canada

Sharp Centre for Design

Alsop Architects

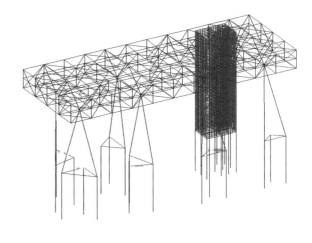

Structural Diagram

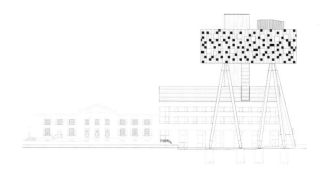

South Elevation

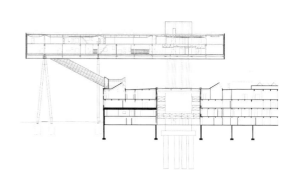

Longitudinal Section

One of the main challenges of the project was to keep the school running as normal during the construction of the volume above the existing buildings. In addition, due to the scarcity of free space on the campus and the proximity of the adjacent buildings, the team could not have a spacious storage area at their disposal. The tall structural columns, weighing up to 20 tons, required immediate installment upon arrival at the site. A straightforward and systematic construction method also allowed neighbors and passers-by to appreciate the process step by step. To obtain the extensive length of the main columns, the architects had to resort to a special technology commonly used in the oil industry and consequently opted for prefabrication off-site. From the installation of the first few columns to the finalization of the structural shell, only four months passed.

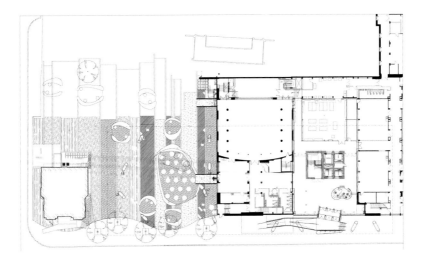

Lower-Level Plan

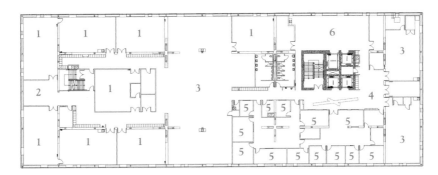

Main-Level Plan

1- Classrooms
2- Critique Room
3- Studios
4- Gallery
5- Office
6- Lounge

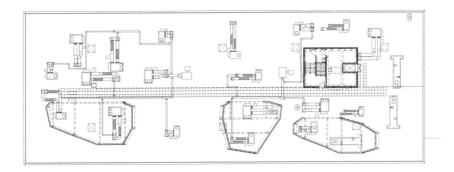

Roof Plan

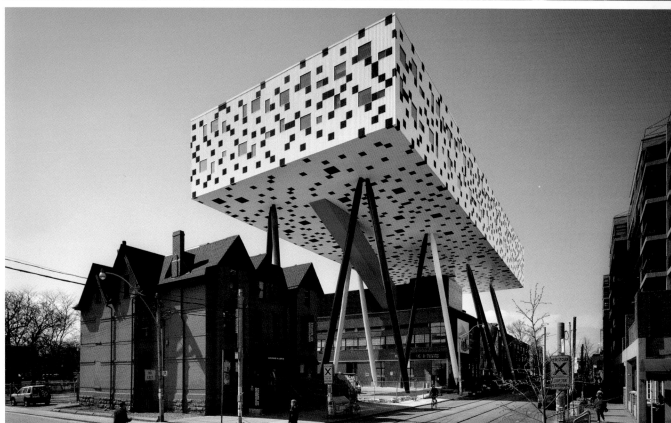

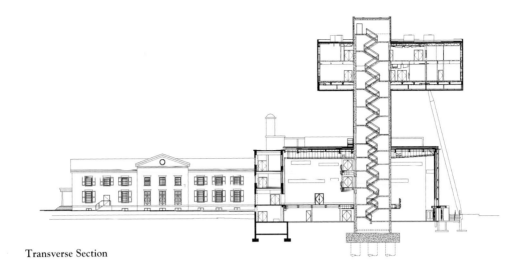

Transverse Section

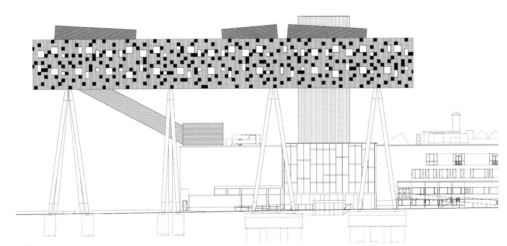

East Elevation

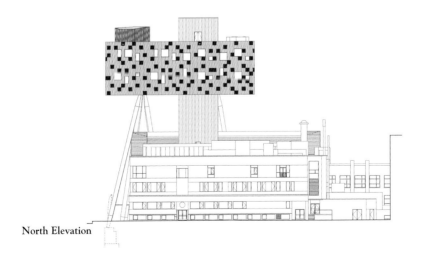

North Elevation

After various adjustments in the design process, the architects settled on a two-floor, 535 foot (163 m)-long volume that runs along the campus from north to south. The building houses new art studios, conference halls, exhibition spaces, a research center, and offices for different faculties. Furthermore, the project succeeds in restructuring the problematic organization of the older buildings by creating a new entrance hall that unifies the circulation spaces and accesses to the various blocks. The extreme climatic conditions of the region, characterized by very cold winters and sweltering summers, necessitated an efficient and sustainable heating and cooling system. In response, architects endowed the volume with a double façade, creating a parametric air pocket that naturally warms or refrigerates the interior space while saving on energy.

Epiphytes

The origin of this singular architectural piece goes back to the election of the city of Rotterdam as European Capital of Culture in 2001. The project was to serve as a visual feature fixed onto the elevator shaft on the roof of the Las Palmas Building, an abandoned industrial warehouse used to host diverse exhibitions throughout that year. One of them, titled *Parasites*, presented a selection of scale models of objects that take advantage of abandoned urban infrastructures by using them as structural support. The exhibit gathered projects by diverse national and international architects, and thanks to the enthusiastic spirit of the cultural encounter, it was decided that one of the projects would be built in real scale. The roof of the Las Palmas Building, located near the city's port, proved an ideal setting for the structure, which was used as the logo for the exhibition. In this way, the Las Palmas Parasite became an architectural prototype that combines the technology of prefabrication with the unique qualities of a custom-made project. The limitations imposed by the size of the elevator shaft required the creation of a small volume, which was painted in bright green and endowed with angular forms to achieve its status as a genuine urban landmark.

Client
Parasites Exhibition

Type of Project
Temporary pavilion

Location
Rotterdam, Netherlands

Total Surface Area
915 square feet (85 m²)

Year of Completion
2001

Photos ©
Anne Bousema, Christian Kahl, Daniel Nicholas, Errol Sawyer

Las Palmas Parasite

Korteknie Stuhlmacher Architecten

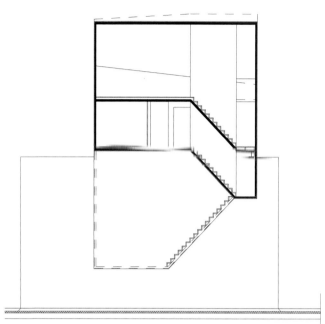

Longitudinal Section

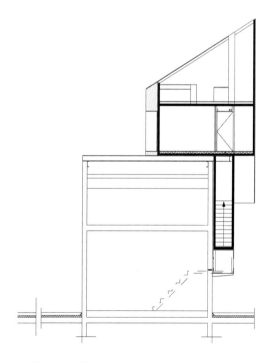

Transverse Section

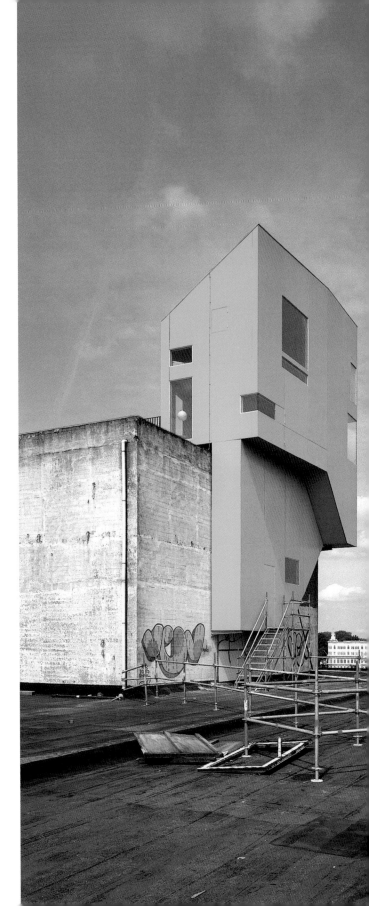

The small pavilion utilizes the reinforced concrete volumes of the roof of the building as structural support elements, and the walls, floors, and ceiling were constructed with laminated wood panels made from recycled European wood. Each element was prefabricated, cut to measure, packed, and delivered to the site as a complete unit ready for assembly, a process that lasted only a few days in spite of harsh winds and which resulted in the first constructed prototype in the Netherlands using this constructive system. The exterior cladding, which serves as thermal insulation, consists of large plywood panels painted bright green. The radical nature of the project offers new possibilities for wood constructions.

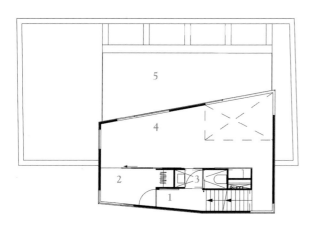

Ground-Floor Plan

1- Entrance
2- Vestibule
3- Services
4- Multiuse Area
5- Terrace

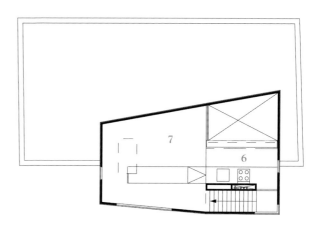

Second-Floor Plan

6- Kitchen
7- Office

The panels used to line the interior of the pavilion were left exposed and untreated, while the openings were treated as simple holes in the wood. Fixed double-glazed windows and ventilation louvers integrated into the wood panels were introduced to avoid the need for window frames. The openings vary in size, character, and position with the aim of emphasizing the variety of stunning views obtained from its location, surrounded by new urban developments and the busy port. In spite of its temporary nature, the building was left in its original place until summer of 2005 and accommodated diverse activities. Because of the rehabilitation plan of Las Palmas, the Parasite was moved and is currently in storage, waiting for new uses and emplacements.

Parasites

This project is located near the Spree River, within the Tiergarten district of Berlin, an area of the city that was almost entirely destroyed by the World War II bombings. The only surviving structure from the attack, a five-story building built in 1907, was the starting point of this project, which combines a police station and a fire station. The original building formed part of a complex comprised of courtyards that divided the different areas and provided the offices with a private interior landscape. Between 1945 and 1991, the surviving structure was used as a railway warehouse because of its proximity to a small railroad, whose eventual shutdown led to the complete abandonment of the building. In 1998, a master plan was designed with the objective of redeveloping this area of the city center and incorporating the building into the new urban fabric. An extension to the building was necessary in order to accommodate the required program. The strategy consisted in creating a compact and efficient project in economic and ecological terms. The architects created a two-story building that leans on the interior façade of the existing building where the former courtyard was located and based its organization on the original structure. The new structure floats one floor above ground, which allowed for the creation of a spacious parking lot for police cars and fire trucks.

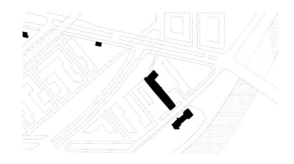

Site Plan

Client
Local government of Berlin

Type of Project
Urban building

Location
Berlin, Germany

Total Surface Area
73,733 square feet (6,850 m²)

Year of Completion
2004

Photos ©
Bitter Bredt Fotografie

Fire and Police Station

Sauerbruch Hutton Architects

Exterior Perspectives

The contrast between old and new was explored through materials and color. The colored-glass skin that envelops the new structure presents an abstract appearance that contrasts with the heavy articulation of the old stone and brick façade. Although the new building functionally depends on the former, a clear contrast can be appreciated between the solidity of the Prussian building and the unconventional, light, and optimistic image lent by the colorful glass annex. The green and red tones of the new skin make reference to the police force and the fire brigade, respectfully, as the recognizable colors of these national institutions. Cladding is composed of glass plates that measure 26 inches (65 cm) in height and vary between 3 feet (1 m) and 8 feet (2.5 m) wide. The joints were left open and the cladding was separated from the main structure in order to ensure a well-ventilated façade.

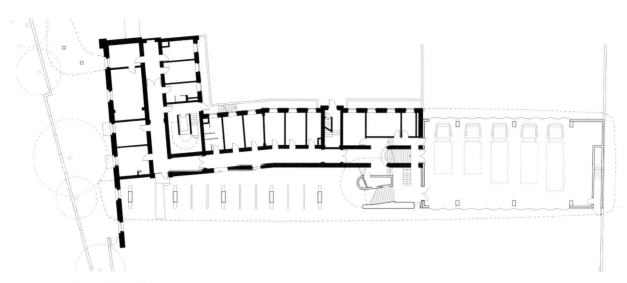

Ground-Floor Plan

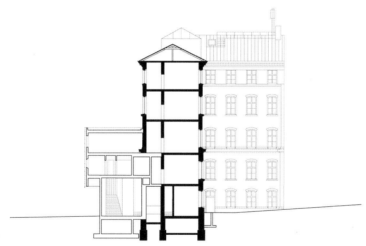

Transverse Section

Side Elevation

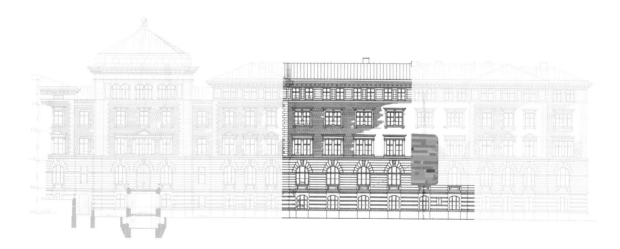

Elevation of the Original Building and of the New Project

The location of the new building was chosen both for its immediate environs and the historical implications of the project. The position of the horizontal extension is reminiscent of the former alignment of courtyards, while the longitudinal extension of the façade relates to the surrounding urban environment. In each case, the combination of the old and new structures was taken advantage of to optimize the functions of the program. Opting for a more traditional public image, the police station was situated along the main façade of the existing building on the north side, while the fire station, which required sophisticated systems and a renewed image, was situated within the new extension. The clean and austere interiors emphasize the architectural qualities of each area.

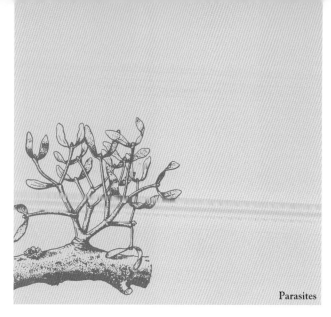

Parasites

This project consists of an addition to a single-family residence in a suburban area of Mexico City characterized by the villa constructions of the 1950s. The clients sought to create a living area for the entire family, but one that would primarily serve as a playing area for their children. Based on the characteristics of the intended users, the architects devised a continuous space without edges and with an enclosed, intimate nucleus that gradually opens up by way of a circular ramp that connects to the garden. The main challenge of the project consisted in reconciling the functional needs of the addition while creating a formal language that unites the addition with existing building. The organic and monolithic form of the new structure sharply contrasts with the orthogonal lines, modulation, and architectural transparency of the original building, emphasizing the idea of an additional, complementary space that is at once unusual and engendered by the original structure itself. The two buildings stand as examples of different architectural styles that link two key periods within Mexican domestic architecture: the onset of the modern movement during the 1950s, and the technological innovations of contemporary architecture.

Client
Private

Type of Project
Residential addition

Location
Mexico City, Mexico

Total Surface Area
377 square feet (35 m²)

Year of Completion
2001

Photos ©
Paul Czitrom, Luis Gordoa, Javier Hinojosa, Paulina García Hubard

Children's Room

Laboratory of Architecture

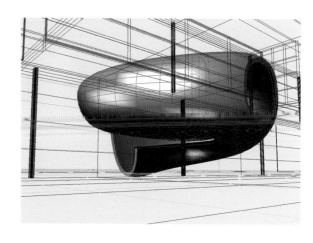

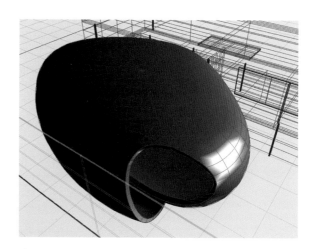

Three-Dimensional Models

Despite its reduced scale, the project posed a considerable challenge to the architectural team. While functional and formal questions were continuously addressed through the entire design process, a thorough investigation of constructive systems was necessary in order to implement the proposal. The building consists of a metallic structure covered with polyurethane foam that was leveled and treated with a polymer coating to obtain a smooth and uniform finish. The project's location in Mexico, a country where the cost of qualified manual labor is still low, was a decisive factor in the construction of this structure with organic forms, which required a certain degree of specialized manual work and craftsmanship. The entire structure was completed in three weeks, thanks to the collaboration of twenty-one laborers and craftsmen who worked an average of twelve hours per day.

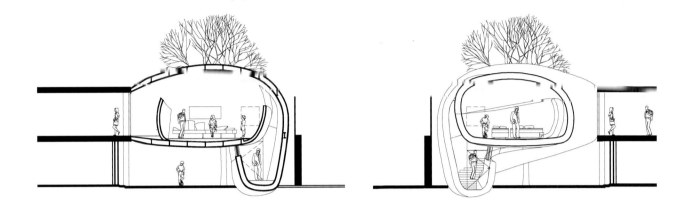

Transverse Sections

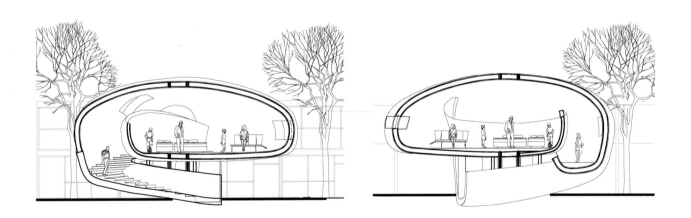

Longitudinal Sections

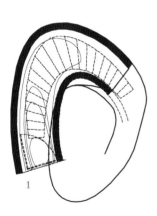

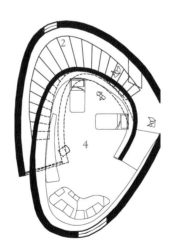

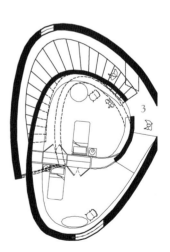

Lower-Level Plan

Mid-Level Plan

Upper-Level
Plan

1- Garden Entrance
2- Ramp
3- Interior Entrance
4- Room

The diaphanous interior is accessed from the first floor of the house, which contains the bedrooms, while a circular ramp leads to the garden. This flexible space, with no edges or defined limits, can be used as a children's bedroom, guest bedroom, or play area. The construction process allowed for an interesting combination of state-of-the-art technology from the United States, such as the laser-cut metallic beams, and the local techniques applied to the finishings. All surfaces were molded and polished by hand to obtain the desired curves and inclinations of the initial design.

Root Systems   Capturing Water   Succulence

Water Control

In the physiology of plants, water is important in many aspects, given that it dissolves all the minerals found in the soil and distributes them throughout the tissue of the plant. In addition, it constitutes one of the fundamental ingredients for photosynthesis and is essential for maintaining the pressure that preserves the rigidity (turgor) of the cell wall. It is also indispensable for the passive existence of protoplasm, the fundamental substance of cells, given that very few tissues can survive if their water content is reduced to 10 percent. Lastly, the presence of water inside the plant that absorbs surrounding heat prevents the event of sudden temperature changes in the protoplasm. In especially dry climates, plants have developed different strategies to optimize the scarce water available. Their objective lies in improving their water supply and in developing systems that permit its storage or prevents its loss.

Root systems | Water storage is optimized primarily through the creation of complex systems of radicles or roots capable of reaching a better source of water supply.

Capturing water | If indeed rain is of crucial importance to plants as the source of humidity in the soil, in general its direct importance is relative. Even so, the morphological features of plants have considerable influence on the microdistribution of precipitation. It is not uncommon to find certain plants in dry climates with morphological structures designed to capture rainwater and channel it to their root systems. The leaves of certain plants, such as aloe vera, ensure that the water that falls upon its leaves is diverted toward the axis or interior of the plant. In arid regions, this phenomenon greatly influences the ability of plants to survive. The flat leaves of thorny acacia extend and act as a funnel, collecting the rain that falls on its foliage and channelling it toward the trunk and roots.

Succulence | This is the most common system of water storage and occurs as a result of the accumulation of water in different organs inside the plant during brief rainy seasons, made possible by the water-storage tissue of plants that enables them to withstand natural droughts. Succulence can occur in roots (*Ceiba parviflora*), stems (cactus, Euphorbia) and leaves (agave, aloe, *Mesembryanthemum*). In the case of *Sedum brevifolium*, two characteristics come together: the phenomenon of succulence and the maximum reduction of surface area, or in other words, the spherical form and the reduction of the leaf surface into a sphere.

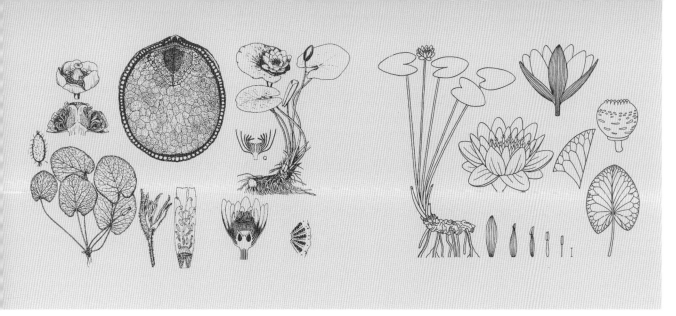

Hydrophyte (Cavities)   Hydrophyte (Long Petioles)

Elimination of water | For plants that live in an environment with a great degree of humidity in the air and soil, the loss of water is not a problem, and on the contrary, these plants posses a structure specially adapted to eliminate excess water. One of the most common strategies consists in increasing transpiration, which, among other things, provokes the loss of water. Many species found in excessively humid climates commonly develop large leaves that favor transpiration. Aquatic plants are especially adapted to live in ponds, streams, lakes, rivers, and lagoons, where terrestrial plants are unable to survive.

Hydrophytes | One of the most extraordinary structural peculiarities shared by the majority of hydrophytic plants—plants that live and grow in water—is the sponginess of their tissue. The large intercellular cavities, full of air, enable many species to float, such as *Aponogeton distachyo* and those of the genus *Nuphar*. In some cases, these very cavities are used to store the gases produced by photosynthesis and respiration, allowing them to live in the water. The *Victoria amazonica*, a well known species of this kind, has leaves that can grow up to 7 feet (2 m) in diameter and, thanks to its concave border that reaches up to 8 inches (20 cm) and to the membrane that partly covers its surface, can float and support up to 11 pounds (5 kg) in weight. In addition, in order to avoid submersion if the water level rises, many aquatic plants develop petioles (stalks that join leafs to stems) that are longer than normal so that they can continue to float on the surface. If the water level continues to rise, the petiole will grow to allow the leaf to reach the water's surface. The *Nuphar*, *Nymphaea* and *Potamogeton* species, among others, possess mechanisms that prevent water from wetting their leaves, such as waxy surfaces that cause water drops to slide off easily, or fuzz that repels water by retaining the droplets above the leaf's surface.

Capturing Water

The Bentsen-Rio Grande Valley State Park is an oasis of wildlife on the lower Rio Grande, in an area used mostly for agricultural purposes. The new World Birding Center occupies 62 acres (25 hectares) that were once reserved for onion plantations and are now being used to recover a wide variety of local species. The park attracts many travelers and tourists in the area, although the majority of visitors are butterfly- or birdwatchers in search of the best view of these species. The project was conceived as a place where visitors could wait for the tram that carries them to the interior of the parks and as a place to learn more about the qualities of this natural habitat. The design incorporates a group of energy-efficient buildings that integrate technology and borrow references from the typical ranch constructions of the region. Three rectangular volumes make up a series of exterior gardens in which diverse ecosystems appropriate to the area are reproduced. Far from imitating the Mexican colonial style common to this region and which a tourist might expect to find, the architectural language of the complex underlines the functional and ecological character of the project. The buildings, simple volumes made of brick and concrete, are covered with a corrugated metallic roof in the form of an arch that serves as a water-capturing device.

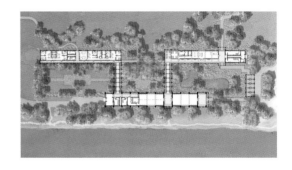

Site Plan

Client
Texas Parks and Wildlife

Type of Project
Visitors center

Location
Mission, Texas

Total Surface Area
23,681 square feet (2,200 m²)

Year of Completion
2004

Photos ©
Hester + Hardaway Photographers

World Birding Center

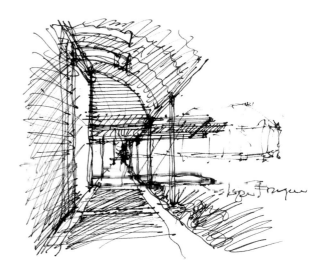

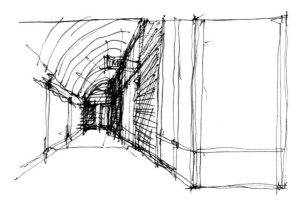

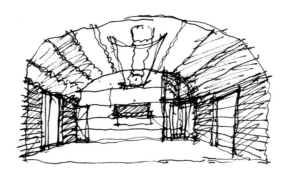

Preliminary Sketches

The program includes observation platforms, an exhibition area, a cafeteria, a library, and the center's administration offices. The spatial layout throughout the three structures that comprise the center, as well as the pedestrian walkways that link them, reinforce the connection to the gardens and the surrounding landscape. The buildings were conceived with the objective of optimizing the energy resources to the maximum. Broad windows on the north façade take advantage of the panoramic views, while the shutters and spacious porches protect the south façade from the intense sunlight that affects the area. The vaulted metallic roofs collect rainwater, which is then channelled to 18 steel storage tanks at different points in the complex, and is later used to water the gardens and supply the center.

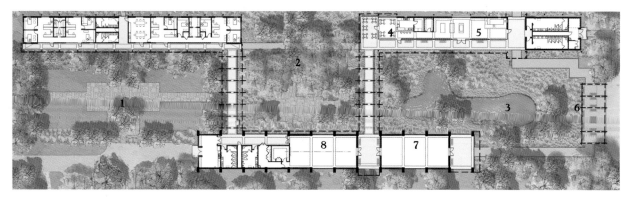

Ground-Floor Plan

1- Entrance Patio
2- Ebony Garden
3- Marsh Garden
4- Cafeteria
5- Library
6- Tram Station
7- Multipurpose Room
8- Gallery

Transverse Sections

Root Systems

This project is located in the Poble Nou neighborhood of Barcelona, one of the areas of the city that has undergone dramatic changes over the last decades. The urban transformations of the city as a result of the 1992 Olympic Games and the 2004 Universal Forum of Cultures have regenerated this old industrial and peripheral neighborhood and transformed it into a dynamic area that has attracted both public and private investment and now is integrated into the city center. During the nineteenth century, textile factories in this area extracted abundant water from the subsoil for their activity. As soon as this industrial regulator disappeared, phreatic levels increased considerably and now water levels can be found at less than 23 feet (7 m) below ground. The new headquarters for Barcelona Activa, a state-run institution that promotes employment, business cooperation, and entrepreneurial spirit, transforms this problem into a feature of the project: two 98-foot (30-m)-deep wells draw a flow of 18,494 gallons (70,0001) per hour at a constant temperature of 64°F (18°C) warmer than the outside air in winter and cooler in summer. The water extracted from the subsoil feeds the hydraulic machine that supplies the energy necessary for climate control, irrigation and sanitary services. This energy system, which also includes a 3,531-cubic-foot (100 m³) pool for storing water, occupies two basement floors underneath the building.

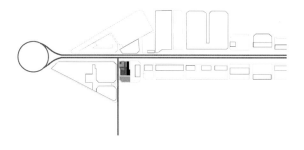

Site Plan

Client
Barcelona Activa

Type of Project
Urban complex

Location
Barcelona, Spain

Total Surface Area
109,049 square feet (10,131 m²)

Year of Completion
2000

Photos ©
Diego Ferrari, Carles Ibarz, Eva Serrats

General Diagram ©
Alison and Peter Smithson

New Barcelona Activa Headquarters

Roldán + Berengué Arquitectos

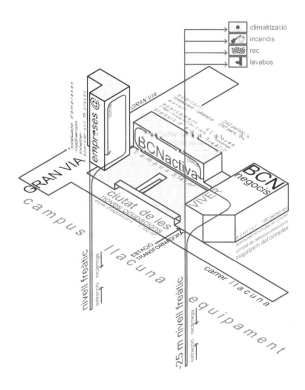

General Diagram

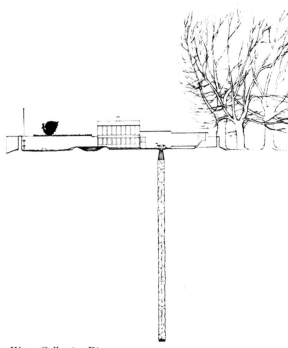

Water Collection Diagram

Organizing the complex entailed a delicate balance between the different programs and new and existing typologies. The project as a whole comprises a mediateque, an auditorium, the corporate headquarters of Barcelona Activa—a growing number of enterprises in an existing building and a new office tower. The different programs within the complex are unified by a plaza partially open to the street and referred to as the campus, which defines the public urban space with a pavilion-door that functions as a screen. This transition area organizes the access to the plaza, the descent to the mediateque, and the entrance to the offices. This concept of transition between public and private, indoor and outdoor, is reflected in the general layout of the project and in the design of the façade, which incorporates a sequence of rectangular balconies across the volume.

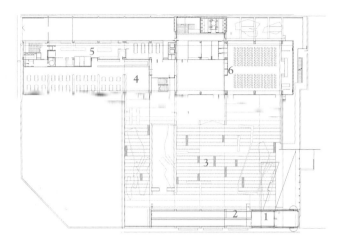

Ground-Floor Plan

1- Entrance
2- Ramp
3- Plaza
4- Restaurant
5- Kitchen
6- Conference Room

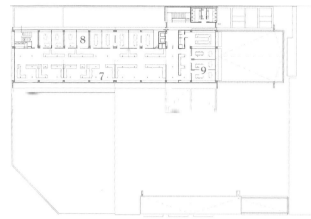

Second-Floor Plan

7- Open Offices
8- Private Offices
9- Meeting Rooms

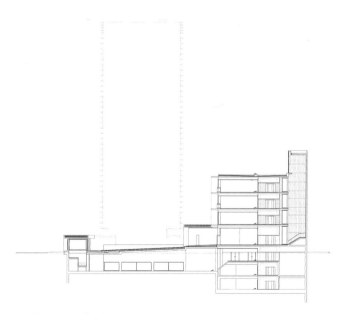

Transverse Section

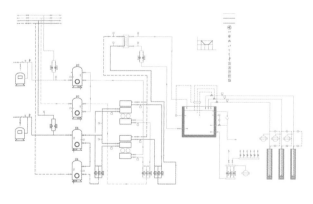

Technical Drawing of the Heating and Cooling System

One of the premises of the project was to achieve a flexible building that would not only adapt to its multiple uses, but that would also allow for different uses in the future. Its accentuated horizontality likens it to the concept of an urban shelf on which other structures can be placed and interchanged according to the necessities of the complex. The entry pavilion incorporates its own advertising, electricity is installed underneath the floors, ceilings integrate mobile light fixtures, and glass panels are equipped with protective surfaces and banners. The architects who defined the project as a "closet" building implemented sobriety to achieve greater versatility and avoid ostentation, precisely what characterized the buildings that once housed industrial production.

Hydrophytes (Long Petioles)

Various atmospheric phenomena within our time have led to the increasing threat of floods across the planet. This is especially the case in regions with deltas, where the ocean and rivers double the threat to numerous communities that commonly inhabit these areas. Nowhere in the world is this a greater preoccupation than in the Netherlands, where the population has withstood centuries of imminent disaster. Nearly one-fourth of the country is land reclaimed from the sea, half of which is situated at or below sea level. The country's vulnerability to the increasing water level, attributed in great part to global warming, has generated a new focus on protecting itself from this threat. For more than fifty years, the Dutch have resorted to high technology to protect themselves from floods. Today, however, campaigns promote architectural solutions to this growing threat, without necessarily depending on the efficiency of large infrastructures. During the 1990s, the government initiated a program for the acquisition of land to be used as floodplains, mainly along the riverbanks. The single-family housing project under discussion here forms part of one of the first prototypes tested by the Dutch and based on one of the oldest solutions to floods: floating architecture.

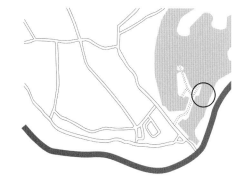

Site Plan

Client
Private

Type of Project
Housing

Location
Maasbommel, Netherlands

Surface Area of Each Residence
700 square feet (65 m^2)

Year of Completion
2005

Photos ©
Factor Architecten

Maasbommel, Netherlands

Houses in Maasbommel

Factor Architecten

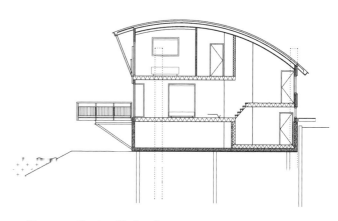

Transverse Section (On Land)

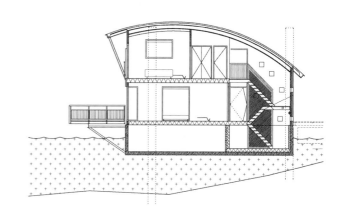

Transverse Section (Floating)

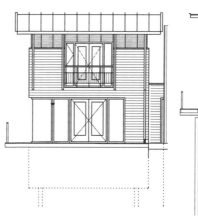

Elevation   Longitudinal Section

Up until a short while ago, construction was prohibited in this flood-prone area. Now these new amphibious houses, designed to float, will rise along with the water level. In contrast to the floating houses anchored along many Dutch canals or those that comprise small villages in Southeast Asia, these are constructed on firm ground, yet are designed to rise with the water level in case of flooding. Constructed with lightweight wood, they rest on a base of hollow granite that allows them to float. The structure, which has no fixed foundations, is simply deposited onto the ground, fastened to 16-foot (5-m) posts with sliding rings that enable the structures to rise and descend with the water level. All of the electrical installations, water pipes and drainage systems are built into flexible tubes inside the fastening posts.

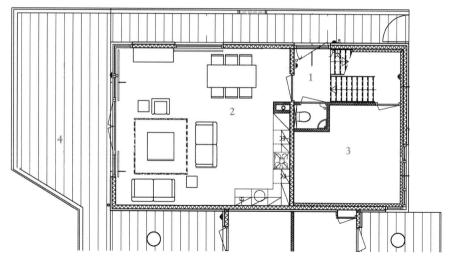

Ground-Floor Plan

1- Entrance
2- Living–Dining–Kitchen
3- Storage Room
4- Terrace

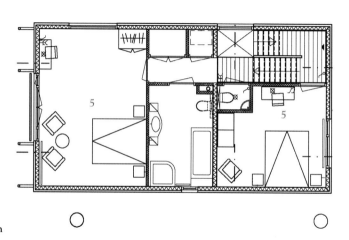

Second-Floor Plan

5- Bedrooms

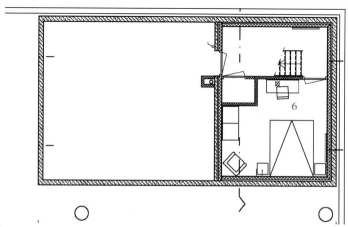

Third-Floor Plan

6- Bedroom

The housing complex is situated on a beautiful plain flooded by one of the country's main waterways: the Maas River. The ingenious residences also respond to the particular need of the Dutch to find habitable space, the Netherlands being the most densely populated country in Europe. Each residential unit has a surface area of 700 square feet (65 m²) distributed over three floors and a compact layout comprised of an integrated living and kitchen area on the ground floor, two bedrooms on the second floor, and a third bedroom on the third floor. During the flooding seasons, residents require a boat to transport them to the dike where they park their cars. Despite the relatively high cost of each residence for a middle-class population like that of Maasbommel, all of the units have already been sold.

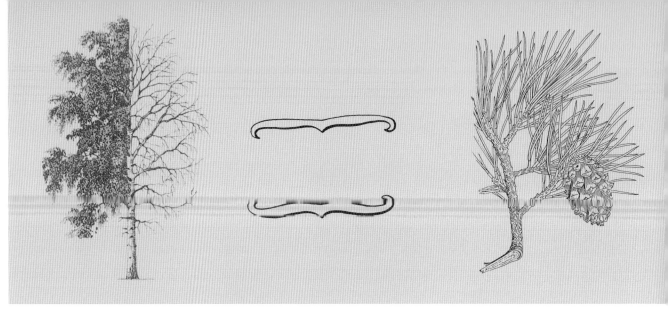

| Fall of the Leaf | Change in Form | Minuscule or Cylindrical Leaves |

Temperature Control

The development process of all plants occurs at an optimum temperature at which their functions are carried out with most efficiency, and cannot continue beyond certain temperature limits. Damage caused by the cold is a consequence of ice formation within the cell wall or intracellular tissue, leaving the plant in a poor state due to mechanical malfunctions. Damage caused by excessive heat, on the other hand, is attributed to the denaturalization of proteins. In any case, either extreme can provoke the plant's death as a result of desiccation. Excess heat can produce excess transpiration, which, along with a lack of water, can result in lethal effects. Excess cold, however, can also provoke dehydration that results from the plant's inability to absorb frozen water. Some plants possess thermal resistance that allows them to withstand extreme temperatures, requiring the development of special devices that avert their effects. These adaptations include: the reduction in size of the exposed surface area to the climatic inclemency, the intense reflection of radiation, the positioning of leaves, and cooling or heating systems through transpiration and insulation.

Fall of the leaf | In temperate latitudes (deciduous plants), this strategy constitutes an adaptation to the cold season that allows the plant to considerably reduce its foliage to avoid

contact with the cold temperature. The *Ephedra fragilis* is a typical example of this, which during summer loses its small leaves and carries out photosynthesis through its green stems.

Change in form | Instead of falling, the leaves of certain plants change in form or position in order to reduce the amount of direct radiation and protect part of the transpiring surface from direct contact with the air. Rosemary leaves, for example, fold upward until the edges join in order for approximately half of each leaf to be protected.

Minuscule or cylindrical leaves | The leaves of the *Erica multiflora* are extremely small and almost cylindrical. Their minimal surface area prevents excessive water loss and still allows for photosynthesis. A similar case is that of many cactaceous plants, in which surfaces are reduced to the point of converting the leaves into spines, or that of conifers like fir or pine trees that bear completely linear, needlelike leaves.

Spherical forms | Another strategy that reduces the degree of insolation on the totality of the plant's surface is the roundness of forms, as exhibited by the hedgehog broom (*Erinacea anthyllis*). Spherical forms adopted by the volume of the plant

Spherical Forms   Stoma Control   Insulation (Lignified Tissues)

itself allow many species to maintain a microclimate and a much cooler internal temperature than that of areas directly exposed to the sun.

Stoma control | If indeed the majority of water given off by the leaves of a plant is lost through stomas or intercellular openings, the principal objective of this is not to facilitate water loss, but to enable the exchange of gases. The coordination between the closure of stomas during drought or extreme heat and their aperture during the process of photosynthesis or respiration is one of the most common physiological adaptations of plants in dry climates. The leaves of sclerophyllous plants, typical of the Mediterranean climate, possess a waterproof coating containing phenol, lignins, and waxes that reduce water loss to a minimum during dry periods (*Quercus ilex*). The presence of small hairs on leaves and stems is another adaptation that controls water loss due to heat, maintaining wind currents above the stomas and thus generating an insulated layer of moist air that protects the plant from desiccation. Stomas sunken into cavities situated below the surface is another strategy employed by many plants that serves to protect the stomas from the air or direct sunlight.

Color and reflectivity | Plants are generally green, although shades tend to vary considerably. In dry climates, the pigmentation of light-colored plants ranging from pale grayish-green to glaucous tones is of great importance in reflecting the sunrays, which would otherwise be absorbed and converted into heat, as in the case of lavender. A similar strategy is the capacity of many sclerophyllous plants to reflect light as a result of the sheen produced by the waxy coating of their leaves.

Insulation | Another strategy proper to cold and hot climates involves the development of materials that facilitate insulation. The buds of plants, insulated by a protective tissue, are one of the mechanisms that offer protection to the organs most sensitive to the cold. Tree bark and, in general, lignified tissues make many plants resistant to extreme temperatures. In some cases, plants preserve dead leaves that no longer perform photosynthesis and are apparently useless, but which actually serve to protect internal tissues sensitive to cold and heat.

Fall of the Leaf

Buildings such as barns and stables tend to be classified as rural architecture—generally vernacular—and consequently not often contemplated within a contemporary framework. In this project, the Studio Pali Fekete Architects team devised a poetic and creative alternative to the traditional manner of storing hay and accommodating a horse stable. The project was based on two contrasting styles: on one hand, the rhythmic rigor and permanence of modernity, and on the other, the constantly changing and rustic component of the Wabi-Sabi, a Japanese aesthetic principle that finds beauty in imperfection. By using the hay as the cladding material for the barn's façade, the perimeter of the building could be used for storage, leaving the interior entirely designated for the stables and other barn facilities. At the end of fall when it is stacked, the hay is freshly cut and green in color. Over the following months and after the hay has dried and adopted a yellowish color, it is removed and used to feed the cattle. In this way, the façade becomes an element that is in constant evolution and the building itself a metaphor for life, birth, and death, themes pertinent to the seasons and the agricultural community.

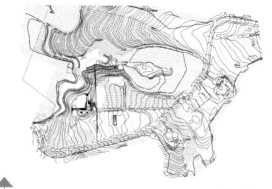

Site Plan

Client
Private

Type of Project
Hay barn and horse stable

Location
Somis, California

Total Surface Area
270 m2

Year of Completion
2004

Photos ©
John E. Linden

Somis Hay Barn

Studio Pali Fekete Architects

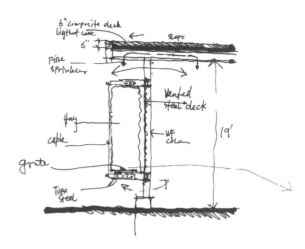

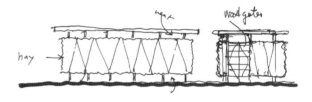

Preliminary Sketches

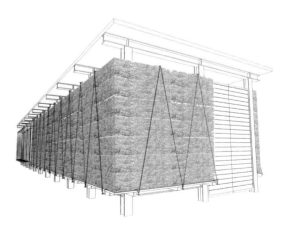

Perspective

The implementation of haystacks as the exterior cladding of the barn's façade not only generates an architectural element with great symbolic character, but also an experience in which the workers themselves participate. The continuous addition and removal of haystacks, apart from the change in color of the hay itself, creates an object that is in constant and dynamic evolution. In order to avoid contact with the humidity of the soil, the hay is stacked onto a shelf situated 3 feet (1m) above the ground that runs along the length of the building's façades and fastened with metallic plates to the structural columns. During the colder months, the hay acts as insulation between exterior and interior.

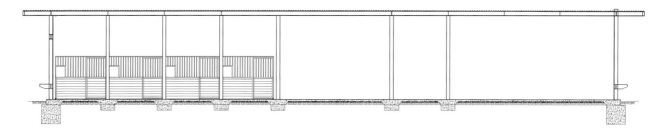

Longitudinal Section

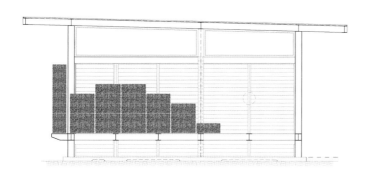

West Elevation

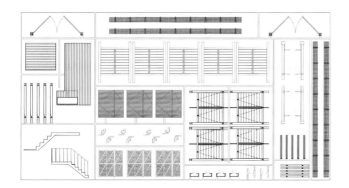

Disposition of Elements

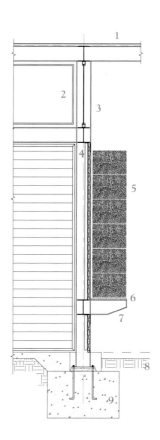

Detail

1- Metal Parquet
2- Ribbon Window
3- Steel Beams
4- Plywood Panels
5- Hay
6- Painted Steel Beam
7- Concrete Slab
8- Stables
9- Concrete Foundation

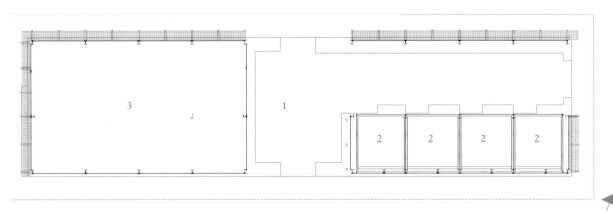

Plan

1- **Entrance**
2- **Stables**
3- **Parking and Storage**

The main access is located in the center of the volume and divides it into two equal parts. While one side houses the stables, the other serves as a tractor garage, a tack room, and a storage area for all other equipment necessary for maintaining the 40 acres (16 hectares) of lemon trees that surround the building. The volume consists of a rectangular structure with a steel framework consisting of a 12-foot-square (3.65 m²) mesh that corresponds to the ideal dimensions of a stable. A window that borders that upper perimeter of the building guarantees natural ventilation, while the expansive eaves of the roof protect the organic cladding from rainfall.

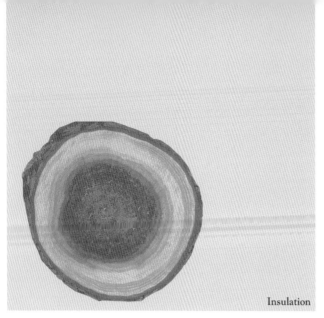

Insulation

The Sfera Building is located in Gion, the famous and popular cultural district of Kyoto, also known as the Geisha district, where it is still possible to catch a glimpse of a geisha in traditional attire amid the multitude of teahouses and private clubs. This image is emblematic of Kyoto, where cultural and architectural tradition make up one of the most important historical areas in Japan. The project consists of a cultural center that houses an art gallery, a bookstore, an exhibition space for design products, a café, and a restaurant. The client's main request was to create a building that respected and maintained a dialogue with the traditional setting and at the same time stood as an innovative, contemporary piece. After designing an interior adapted to the necessities of the program, the architects were challenged with creating a façade that incorporated an engraved pattern of cherry-tree leaves. The idea was inspired by the Japanese tradition of design based on the observation of nature, and particularly by the traditional screens made of bamboo, wood, or paper. Separated from the main volume, the façade creates an air pocket that acts as thermal insulation and constitutes a significant energy-saving feature. The seamless arrangement of panels produces a monolithic appearance from the exterior and a soft and tranquil atmosphere within the building.

Site Plan

Client
Shigeo Mashiro, Ricordi & Sfera Co.

Type of Project
Offices and cultural center

Location
Kyoto, Japan

Total Surface Area
12,917 square feet (1,200 m²)

Year of Completion
2003

Photos ©
Johan Fowelin, Takeshi Nakasa, Ricordi & Sfera Co.

Sfera Building

Claesson Koivisto Rune

Preliminary Sketches of the Façade, the Public Areas, and the Restaurant

In order to create the panels, cherry-tree leaves were picked and arranged in random order, photographed, digitalized, and manipulated to obtain a repetitive pattern formed by perforations with different diameters. This pattern was then perforated into fine titanium panels that were mounted onto an iron structure 7 feet (2 m) from the interior façade. Depending on the angle of light, the building transforms throughout the day. Passing rays of sunlight cast a distinct and varying pattern of leaves projected onto the interior surfaces, producing a subdued and comforting illumination. At night, green lights situated behind the metal panels cause the building to glow from within, likening it to that of a large Japanese lantern.

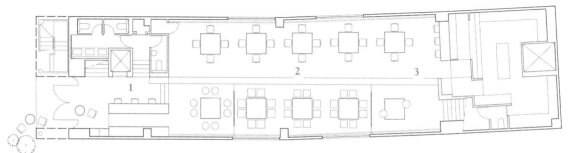

Ground-Floor Plan

1- Service Entrance
2- Restaurant
3- Bar

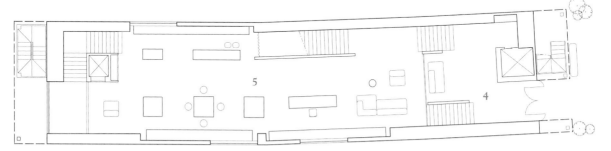

Second-Floor Plan

4- Main Entrance
5- Main Lobby

Third-Floor Plan

6- Exhibition Space
7- Mediateque
8- Storage

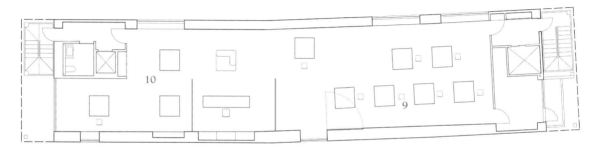

Fourth- and Fifth-Floor Plan

9- General Offices
10- Administration Offices

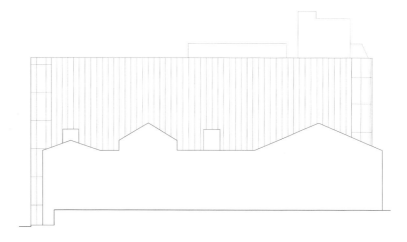

Side Elevation

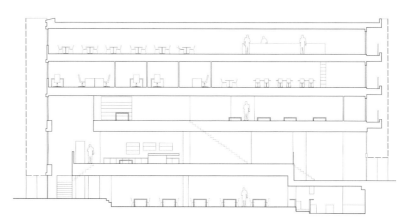

Longitudinal Section

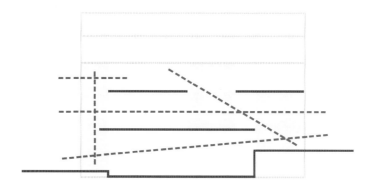

Diagram Showing Paths of Natural Light

Although the project did not involve any structural complications, the internal layout required careful planning. The elongated shape responds to the narrow proportions of the plot and obliged the architects to create an internal distribution that optimized the sources of natural light situated at both extremes. The internal space is a three-dimensional jigsaw puzzle reminiscent of cellular structures. Thanks to the triple-height ceilings, the different use areas flow organically into one another. A continuous staircase running throughout the three floors reinforces this fluidity and emphasizes the directionality of the space.

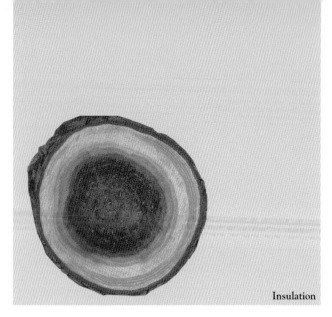

Insulation

This project was submitted to the competition for the new head-quarters of the Mill Art Center, a cultural complex located in downtown Hendersonville, North Carolina. Comprising over 107,639 square feet (10,000 m²), the complex was to accommodate a theater seating 1,200, a children's museum, art galleries, classrooms, artist studios, and administration offices. The architects' proposal took into account the traditional architectural features of the area as well as the landscape of the region. The concept of the project for the cultural center is based on the traditional North American porch, chosen for its qualities as an element that joins interior and exterior and as a common meeting space in American residences. This feature is taken to an urban scale and extended throughout the building as an architectural element that encourages the outdoor activities of the center. In addition to becoming a formal characteristic of the project visible from diverse areas of the city, and from any interior space of the building, the skin that wraps around the composition is a cladding designed to provide shade and protective insulation from external climatic changes.

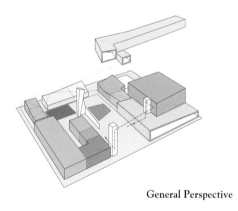

General Perspective

Client
Mill Center for the Arts

Type of Project
Cultural center (project)

Location
Hendersonville, North Carolina

Total Surface Area
109,792 square feet (10,200 m²)

Year of Completion
2005

Photos ©
Pugh + Scarpa

Mill Center for the Arts

Pugh + Scarpa, Eskew + Dumez + Ripple

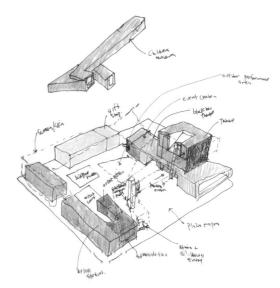

General Sketch

Breakdown of the Façade

Inspired by an image of the forests of the Carolina mountain range that delimits the city's metropolitan area and constitutes a predominant feature of the urban landscape, the cladding is comprised of a system of ionized metal panels engraved with a perforated composition of local tree species. The panels are mounted onto a series of frames that are anchored to, yet separate from, the building façade, transforming into an extensive porch that borders the entire building and creating a light filter for both interior and exterior. Thanks to the perforations of the panels, which make up 28 percent of the metallic surface, the cladding functions as a large screen that allows subtle views into the interior of the building.

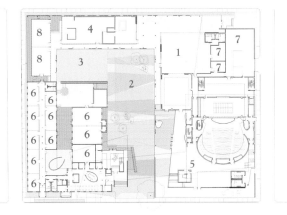

Ground-Floor Plan

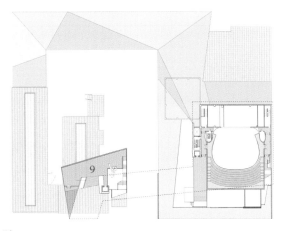

Second-Floor Plan

Third-Floor Plan

1- Entrance Lobby
2- Open-Air Theater
3- Garden
4- Art Gallery
5- Theater
6- Studios
7- Services
8- Classrooms

9- Children's Museum

10- Children's Museum

The flexibility and interaction between the different activities that inspire the project are obtained through the creation of a volume that revolves around a central exterior space and includes the most important public areas: a landscaped plaza and an open-air theater. The ground floor accommodates activities with larger audiences, such as the theater, classroom, and galleries, while the upper levels, which twist and turn into angular forms, house the children's museum. At night, the lighting behind the cladding transforms the complex into a theatrical backdrop. Likening that of a constellation, light is projected through the metallic panels, emphasizing the functional, dynamic, and experimental character of the project.

Pyramid Shape

Sprouters

Extreme Conditions

In some cases, plants have had to adapt to unusual or extreme conditions. These situations can be provoked by weather conditions or simply form part of the environment in which the plants live. Outlined here are the adaptations to four distinct situations: the presence of snow, the onset of fire, and the effects of water and wind on plants.

WIND | Snow can be harmful or beneficial to plants:
Pyramid shape | The branches of trees can break under the weight of snow, especially if a snowstorm is followed by heavy winds, or if cold rain falls on vegetation already laden with snow. Trees with asymmetrical treetops can shift from their vertical position and bend in response to the weight of snow, resulting in the accumulation of snow to the point of breaking the tree. Pyramid-shaped treetops, such as those of fir trees, facilitate the fall of accumulated snow during winter.

FIRE | Fire requires fuel, oxygen, and a source of heat that provides the initial energy to trigger combustion. Cellulose and lignin are the main substances of a plant considered to be highly flammable. Vegetation is flammable, and in places where the risk of fire is high, plants have developed different mechanisms to reduce their flammability.

Resprouting species | These plants are capable of resprouting thanks to the resistance of their roots or trunk. A great majority of Mediterranean species resprout vigorously after being struck by fire. Although their leaves may be completely destroyed, the preservation of vital tissues allowing them to resprout makes them resistant to fires. This is made possible by the insulating characteristics of bark and the location of the organs underground. The cork oak is one example. One month after a fire, the trunk and branches can already reach 8 inches (20 cm) in length. Being a poor conductor of heat, the soil also offers protection to the parts of a plant underneath its surface. The Kermes oak (*Quercus coccifera*) disappears from above the ground, yet resprouts from the root.

STRONG WATER CURRENTS | The adaptation of plants to strong currents of water basically consists in reducing the mechanical resistance to the current.
Dissected leaves | Many plants in fluvial environments threatened by floods (*Phragmites communis*) strengthen their root system by producing dissected leaves or narrow, linear leaves. Certain species even produce submerged leaves that are different from those above the water's surface, like the leaves of the

Dissected Leaves   Flexibility   Adaptation to the Topography

Ranunculus aquatilis, which are highly segmented underwater but flat and treble-shaped when floating on the water's surface.

Flexibility | In places with seasonal flooding, it is common to find woody shrubs that are highly flexible. These species, especially those of the genus *Salix*, fall over without snapping and straighten back up once flooding passes.

No resistance | Another, very different strategy that enables many plants to survive strong water currents is the absence of resistance, and flowing with the current until reaching the backwater. This is the case of duckweed, or *Lemna minor*, which floats on the surface while its roots remain lose and unanchored to the bottom, providing it with a mobility that is unusual within the vegetal kingdom.

STRONG WINDS | The strategies in response to wind currents are very similar to those of water, yet take different factors into account.

Adaptation to the topography | A similar adaptation exists between plants exposed to water currents and those subjected to harsh winds. By adapting to the topography of the terrain, the plant creates minimum resistance and can grow safely without breaking or drying up. Tree species such as the *Pinus mugo* or *Pinus nigra*, which in favorable condi-

tions may reach several yards in height, grow in the form of low shrubs at high mountain altitudes.

Mobility with the wind | Dune and coastal vegetation is another example of the creeping type, which enables plants to resists the lashing of salted sea winds. In areas where wind is frequent, certain plants have learned to take advantage of it as a mode of transportation. Tumbleweed, or *Eryngium campestre*, in particular, which often appears in films depicting the American West, detaches its stem from the roots during the fall and embarks on a journey that will lead it to colonize new territories.

Pyramid Shape

The construction of this small refuge for mountain climbers forms part of an exploration and communication program between two regions: the Terska Valley in Italy and Breginjski Kot in Slovenia. Financed by the PHARE fund of the European Union, the project encourages the promotion and development of small businesses that stimulate communication between different cultural regions of the Union. In addition to the shelter, the program includes information centers and the creation of biking and hiking trails. The objective of the project was to create an architectural structure in a strategic spot along this route that would serve as a refuge for local hikers. Alpine architecture is commonly associated with isolated structures that respect the fragility of the natural surroundings and which are highly resistant to specific and severe climatic conditions, as well as the scarcity of water. Instead of turning to high technology for solutions, the project implements a simple and economic architectural strategy devised through a careful technical study. A close collaboration with the structural engineer was crucial in understanding the different behaviors of an object exposed to such conditions. The design is based on a clear evaluation of the location and its topography, which guided the architect in choosing the right spot for the refuge, as well as determining the right form, structure, and construction method.

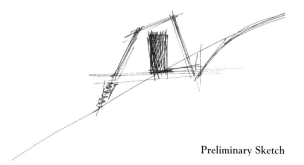

Preliminary Sketch

Client
Breginj Tourist Development Association

Type of Project
Refuge

Location
Mount Stol, Slovenia

Total Surface Area
118 square feet (11 m²)

Year of Completion
2002

Photos ©
Blaz Budja, Miha Kajzelj

Mountain Bivouac

Miha Kajzelj

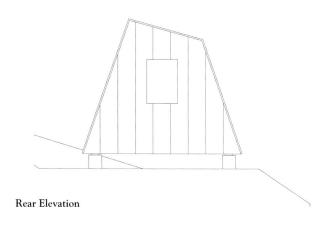

Rear Elevation

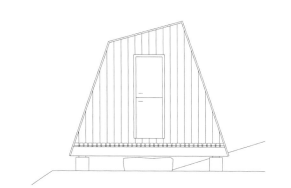

Front Elevation

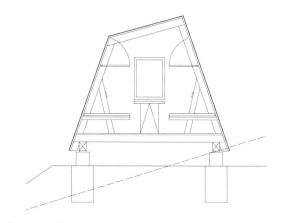

Transverse Section

The refuge is situated on the crest of the mountain where the trail meets the mountain range, on a small, excavated embankment that serves to protect two sides of the cabin. The exposed surfaces are the entrance façade, which faces the trail, and the roof. The characteristics of the site allowed for the structure to be easily adapted to the topography, offering protection from harsh winds and making the most of panoramic views. The very shape of the building, which adapts to the natural inclination of the mountain and the direction of the winds, prevents the accumulation of snow and facilitates its elimination. Once the aerodynamic shape was devised, the refuge was prefabricated and mounted on-site by two mountain climbers.

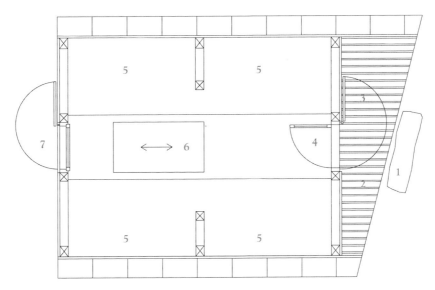

Floor Plan

1- Stone Step
2- Deck Terrace
3- Outer Door
4- Inner Door
5- Sleeping Platform
6- Folding Table
7- Rear Window

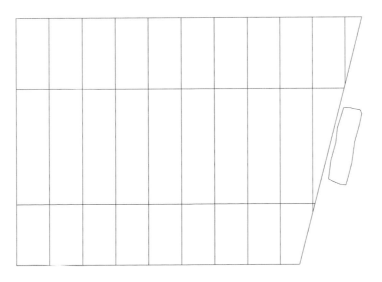

Roof Plan

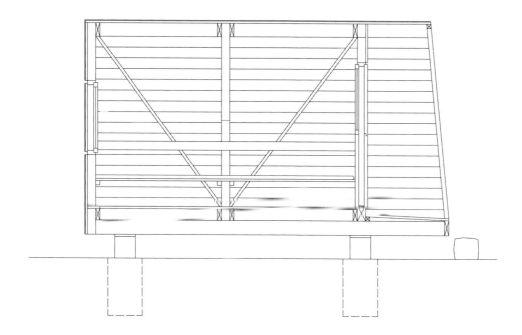

Longitudinal Section

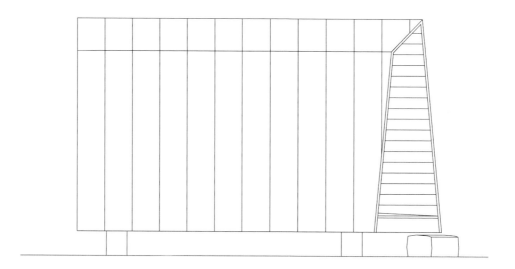

Elevation

After the exterior design of the cabin, a variation of the traditional tent, was settled, the interior had to be approached
in relation to the essential characteristic of the project: maximum usable space with minimum elements and construction materials. The interior design consists of two benches
situated along the two longitudinal sides of the refuge, which
can also be used as sleeping platforms. A central table functions as a studio and eating area. The exterior is entirely
clad in aluminum panels that offer great resistance, while
the interior is predominantly lined in wood to provide thermal insulation and a sense of warmth. The simplicity and
efficiency of this prototype allows for the future construction of similar modules in locations with similar climatic
conditions.

Dissected Leaves

The extreme conditions that characterize the landscape of Abiquiu, New Mexico, the town in which this house is located, make it a particularly remarkable place. It is situated within a semidesertic valley formed by the Chama River and dominated by high temperatures in summer and strong snowfall in winter. Abrupt changes in temperature and the morphology of the region generate continuous winds that lash the site and hamper the growth of protective vegetation, except for the presence of shrubs that have gradually adapted to the severe climate and rarely grow more than 3 feet (1m) in height. The very name of the house, Turbulence, reveals the determining feature of the project. The objective here was to create an object that, through its form and finishings, would allow wind to pass through it without affecting the structure. Situated on a plateau that acts as a pedestal for the new structure, the house enjoys stunning panoramic views. The twisted volume was devised with sophisticated 3D programs and incorporates a large hole that pierces the structure from one side to the other through which strong winds can pass. The white aluminum sheets easily adapt to the aerodynamic form of the structure and also obtain a high degree of insulation, greatly reducing the house's energy consumption.

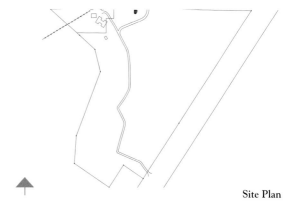

Site Plan

Client
Private

Type of Project
Single-family house

Location
Abiquiu, New Mexico

Total Surface Area
2,906 square feet (270 m²)

Year of Completion
2003

Photos ©
Paul Warchol, Steven Holl Architects

Turbulence House

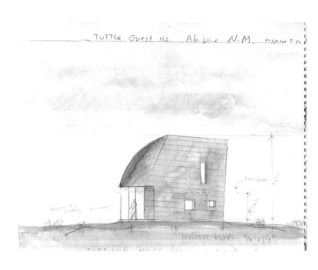

Preliminary Drawings

Wind variations typical of the region were studied with the aid of 3D design programs in order to design the structural framework of the building. The A. Zahner Company, based in Kansas City, was responsible for the prefabrication of the metallic parts that were to be assembled on-site in as little time and with as few workers as possible. In this way, the intervention and effects on the surrounding landscape would be reduced to a minimum. The roof is partially clad with photovoltaic panels that generate an average of 1 kilowatt-hour per day, enough to meet the basic electricity needs of the house. Sufficient space on the roof was provided for the installation of additional panels and a production of up to 3 kilowatt-hours a day.

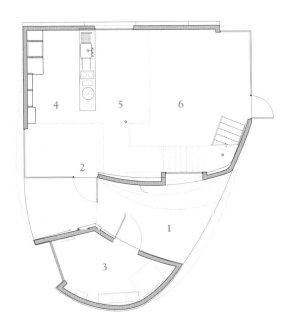

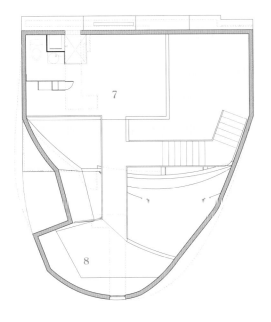

Ground-Floor Plan

1- Exterior Vestibule
2- Entrance
3- Storage Room
4- Kitchen
5- Dining Room
6- Living Room

Second-Floor Plan

7- Bedroom
8- Studio

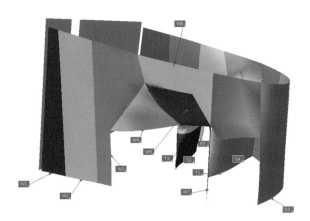

3D Models

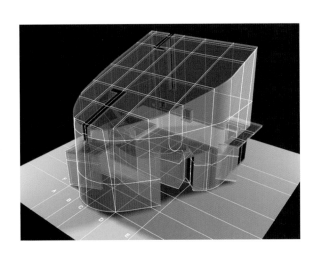

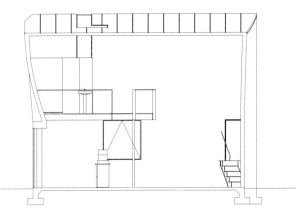

Transverse Section

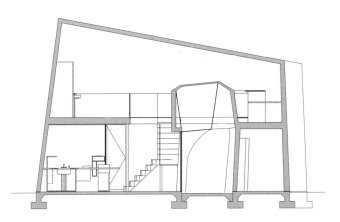

Longitudinal Section

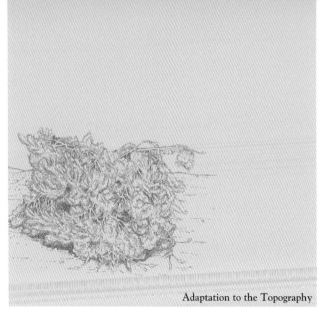

Adaptation to the Topography

The Svalbard Archipelago in the Arctic Ocean constitutes the most northern point of Norway. Only three of its numerous islands are inhabited—by miners and fishermen—thanks to the harsh climate, marked by perpetual snowfall. Although the northern Atlantic current warms the Arctic area and keeps the waters clean and navigable for most of the year, 60 percent of the archipelago is covered by glaciers and snow. Svalbard is situated north of the Arctic Circle, which means that the midnight sun lasts from April 20 to August 23, and twenty-four-hour darkness from October 26 to February 15. This project, whose design resulted from a public contest, consists of an extension that quadruples the size of the already existing university building and research center of Longyearbyen, as well as a new museum. The building is by far the largest in the archipelago. Different strategies were implemented to adapt the project to such a difficult environment, one of them being the elevation of the entire structure onto pillars to prevent the frost that accumulates around the building from melting. The primary material used for both the structure and cladding is wood, for its insulating qualities, while the exterior copper cladding provides additional insulation and adapts to the geometry of the building.

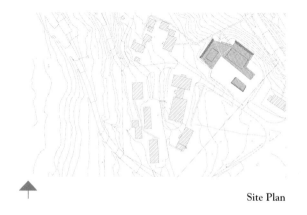

Site Plan

Client
Statsbygg, the Norwegian Directorate of Public Construction and Property

Type of Project
University and museum

Location
Longyearbyen, Svalbard, Norway

Total Surface Area
91,493 square feet (8,500 m²)

Year of Completion
2005

Photos ©
Nils Petter Dale

Svalbard Research Centre

Jarmund/Vigsnæs Architects

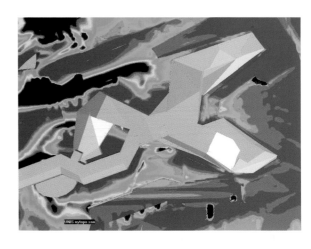

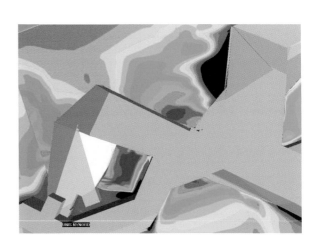

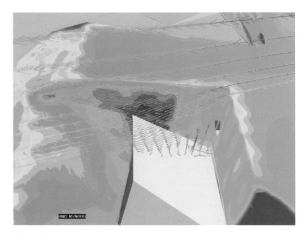

Digital Studies

An insulating copper skin sheathes the entire edifice, its shape adapting to the movements of the wind and the fall of snow. In response to the severe climate, the architects used digital simulation to reproduce the effects of wind, the accumulation of snow in crucial areas of the building, the incidence of sunlight, and other determining factors. During the design process, the cladding was modified in form and size in adjusting to the climate and other changes in the program. Digital 3D models and a 1:50 scale model of the entire complex aided in achieving a building fully adapted to the environment, and one that turns the adverse climate in which it is located into the underlying theme of the design.

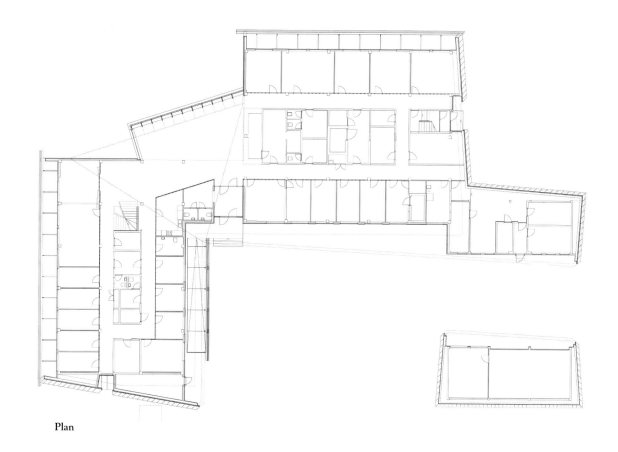

Plan

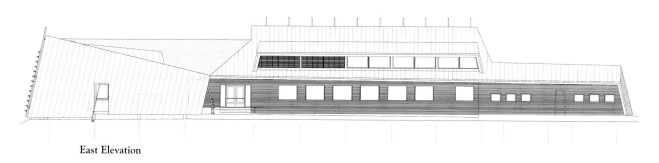

East Elevation

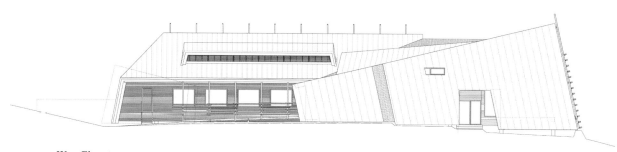

West Elevation

One of the challenges of this project was to generate a series of active public spaces and a circulation system connecting the different areas that together were capable of offering comfort and vitality even during the coldest months of the year. The building is conceived as a luminous and warm interior space that serves as a meeting place during the dark and cold winter. The pine used to line the interior spaces lends a warm atmosphere and also adapts to the complex geometry of the volume. The use of bright colors—uncommon to the natural surroundings—also contributes to the quality of the space the architects sought. The circulation system, apart from linking the different areas in the most efficient manner possible, was also conceived to create comfortable and sheltered areas from which to enjoy the stunning exterior landscape.

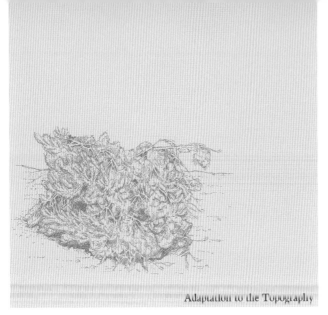

Adaptation to the Topography

The European Southern Observatory (ESO) is a facility sponsored by eleven countries from the European Union, dedicated to astronomical investigation and responsible for the Very Large Telescope (VLT), a series of four telescopes that work independently or together to constitute the most powerful terrestrial telescope on the planet. The installations of the telescope and the research center are situated at the top of Paranal Mountain north of the Atacama Desert in Chile. This project, located in the lower part of the valley dominated by the mountain, is designated as the lodging place for the staff of scientists and engineers who visit the site throughout the year. The harsh climate of the region was the determining factor in the design of the project. Atacama is known as the most arid of all deserts in the world, a condition partially due to its latitude and to the Andes Mountains, which act as a barrier to the influx of humidity from the Atlantic and the Amazon. In fact, Atacama has withstood periods of up to four hundred years without rainfall in its most central area, making it a place marked by intense sunlight, extreme dryness, high-speed winds, notable fluctuations in temperature, and a high risk of earthquakes. In light of this, the project was to serve as an oasis of rest and relaxation for the hotel guests.

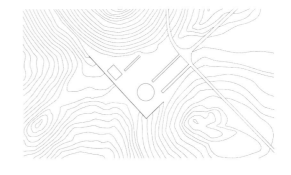

Site Plan

Client
European Southern Observatory

Type of Project
Hotel

Location
Cerro Paranal, Chile

Total Surface Area
129,167 square feet (12,000 m²)

Year of Completion
2002

Photos ©
Roland Halbe

Cerro Paranal, Chile

ESO Hotel

Auer + Weber Architekten

General Views

The primary objectives of the project were to have a minimum impact on the environment and to offer a relaxing atmosphere to the occupants by offsetting the extreme weather conditions of the site. The extensive, 129,167 square foot (12,000 m²) volume is embedded in a natural depression in the terrain, which acts as an artificial supporting wall. By burying a large part of the building in the ground, the breathtaking views toward the Pacific Ocean remain unobstructed, while the building is granted thermal insulation and protection from drastic temperature changes and strong winds. The project emphasizes the natural character of the terrain, deliberately contrasting it with the high-tech image of the telescopes situated along the crest of the mountain.

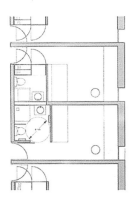

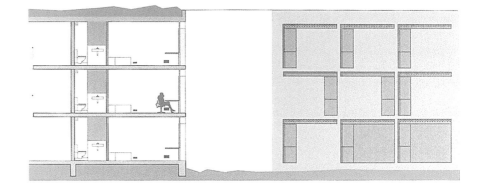

Plan, Section, and Elevation

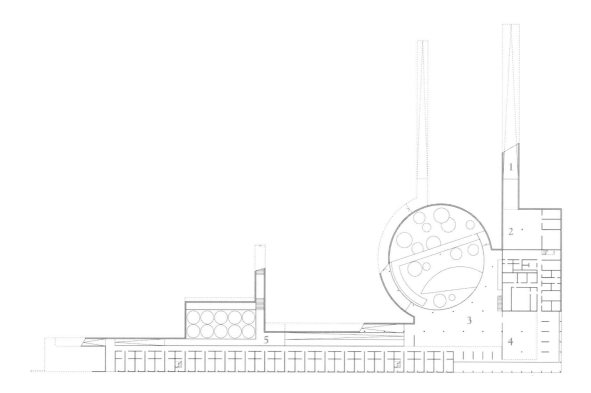

Ground-Floor Plan

1- Entrance Ramp
2- Reception Area
3- Lobby
4- Pool
5- Guest Rooms
6- Interior Patio
7- Library
8- Guest Rooms

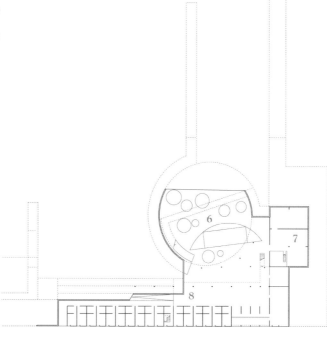

Second-Floor Plan

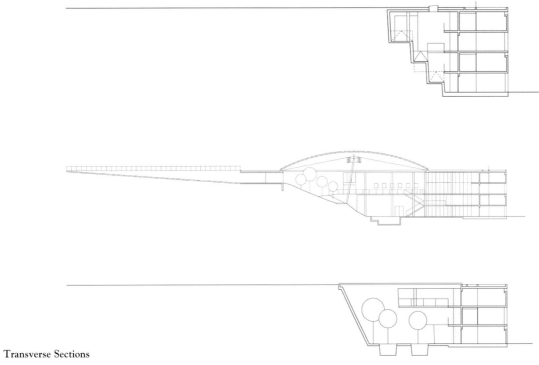

Transverse Sections

The complex incorporates 120 rooms, a bar, lounge area, pool, fitness center, and library. From the access platform, located on the roof and completely integrated with the surrounding landscape, the only element that gives away the existence of a buried structure is a glass dome that rises above the horizontal landscape. A steel skeleton with a diameter of 115 feet (35 m) supports the translucent glass dome, creating a large central courtyard around which the diverse activities of the hotel are organized. This constitutes the focal point of the project where the common areas converge, while the guest rooms, situated along the length of the building, look out toward the expansive desert.

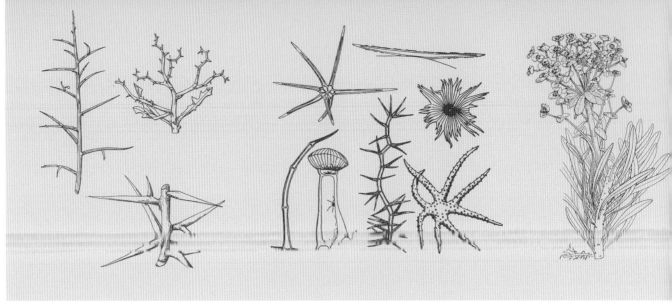

Needles   Trichomes   Latex

Defense

In order to stay alive and ensure their survival as a species, plants must struggle for the possession of soil to preserve their vital space. In response to the threat of a wide variety of vertebrate and invertebrate herbivores, plants have developed a range of physical and chemical defense mechanisms.

Spines | The presence of spines or spikes can dissuade animals from approaching a plant, thus avoiding the risk of getting injured. Examples of plants with spines and thorns include the gorse, the rose, and the blackberry. Often, the spines of numerous species harden with the accumulation of inorganic crystalline substances, such as calcium or silica and, in order to be effective, must be sharp and relatively hard enough to penetrate the skin of an animal. Occasionally, the leaf itself adopts the form of a narrow, round, or pointed spine, as occurs with the barberry (*Berberis vulgaris*). In other instances, the spine may correspond only to part of the leaf, often the point, as with the holly plant or the Kermes oak. The Holm oak, for example, develops thorny leaves only at a young age when the plant is still too small and fragile to protect itself from predators. During its growth, the tree preserves thorns only on the leaves closest to the ground, while the remaining leaves adopt rounded edges and cease to be prickly.

Trichomes | Many plants have developed defense mechanisms against the attack of insects by acquiring an unpleasant taste or producing urticating substances or alkaloids that make them poisonous. This phenomenon is due mainly to the presence of trichomes—small hairs on the epidermis of a plant—capable of secreting substances harmful to insects and other predators, and which in humans can produce irritation. A widely known example of this is the *Urtica dioica*, or stinging nettle, which possess an irritant chemical in its trichomes. In the same way, the cotton plant and soybean, thanks to the multiple trichomes of their leaves, are able to ward off grasshoppers and other predators.

Latex | Latex is another repellent widely produced by many plants. The substance is a whitish, glutinous emulsion with suspended rubber, alkaloid, or terpene particles. In most cases, latex is irritating and distasteful. A total of twenty families and approximately twelve thousand species produce latex, among them blackberry and euphorbia. The presence of aromatic oils, not only for their taste, but also for their strong odor, can also discourage predators from eating the leaves of certain species, which is the case in many aromatic plants typical of the Mediterranean.

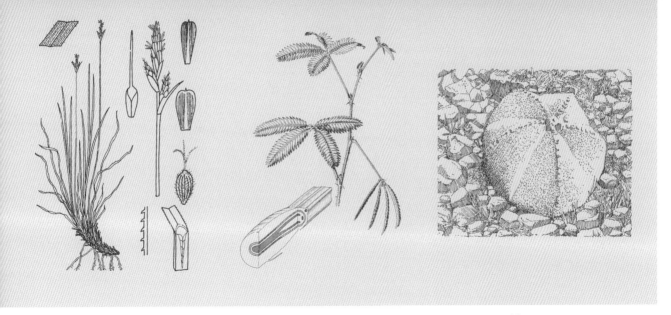

Silica   Sensitive Plant   Mimesis

Silica | Graminaceous species resist depredation by accumulating large quantities of silica in their leaves and stems, a substance that provokes a significant wearing of the teeth in herbivores. Their leaves are also capable of growing from the base of the plant as opposed to the apex, as occurs with most plants, allowing them to resprout once cut down.

Symbiosis with herbivores | An interesting defense mechanism allows certain plants to establish mutually beneficial relationships with certain species of herbivores. This is the case of plants that generate sweet substances, such as nectar, to attract ant colonies that feed on the nectar and serve to defend the plant from being attacked by other herbivores.

Sensitive plant | It is difficult for plants to avoid being attacked by herbivorous animals by concealing their leaves, given that these must always be extended to capture the necessary sunlight for photosynthesis. Nevertheless, certain species have managed to overcome this difficulty, like the sensitive plant (*Mimosa pudica*), which reacts to the physical contact of an insect, for example, by folding its leaves upward and reducing itself to a bundle of branches that are

consequently of no interest to the animal. This phenomenon is generated by variations in turgor of specific cells located at the base of the leaves.

Lignified tissues | Woody tissues not only provide insulation and structural rigidity to a plant, but also protect the most vulnerable tissues of the plant from predators.

Mimesis | Lastly, it is worth mentioning a strategy which, although more common in the animal realm, is also present in the plant kingdom. Mimesis is a system of defense that implements camouflage in partially or entirely integrate a living thing into the surrounding environment. The plant develops physical characteristics that prevent it from being detected by predators, either permanently or temporarily. Plants pursue two forms of mimesis, disappearing completely or transforming into an unappetizing object for the enemy. A desert cactus (*Astrophytum myriostigma Lemaire*), for example, adopts a spherical form with a crackled gray surface that resembles the surrounding rocks to such a degree that even when wet by rain, it darkens in the same manner as do the rocks.

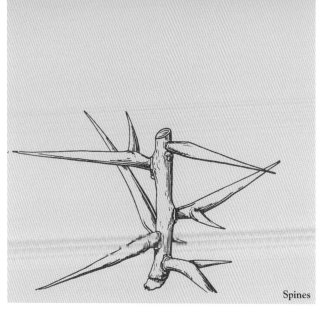

Spines

The site chosen for the construction of the new Dutch Embassy in Poland is located very near to the Lazienki Park, an area of the city characterized by its rural atmosphere and its abundance of residences and embassies. Commissioned by the Ministry of Foreign Affairs of the Netherlands, the project was to reflect the concepts of openness and transparency and incorporate the chancellery and ambassador's residence within the same building. The main challenge consisted in reconciling the formal aspects in relation to the image, solidity, and security that an embassy program entails, with the desire to integrate the building into the surrounding landscape. The only historical building nearby was built by the Dutch Baroque architect Tylman van Gameren, whose work had a great influence on Polish architecture during the seventeenth century and served as a reference point for the design process of the new embassy, especially his mastery in interpreting Baroque in such an austere manner. The chancellery and residence are situated in two independent buildings that relate to the exterior in different ways, but which are linked to each other by an ornamental gate with vegetal motifs that encloses the complex. This organic element, which at times is separate from the building and at other times forms part of the façade, serves as an important element of security as well as a decorative connection between the architecture and the natural surroundings.

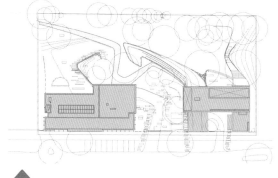

Site Plan

Client
Ministry of Foreign Affairs

Type of Project
Embassy, chancellery, and residence

Location
Warsaw, Poland

Total Surface Area
37,674 square feet (3,500 m²)

Year of Completion
2004

Photos ©
Christian Richters

Dutch Embassy

Erick van Egeraat Associated Architects

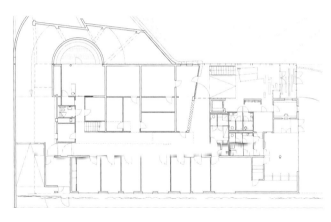

Ground-Floor Plan of Chancellery

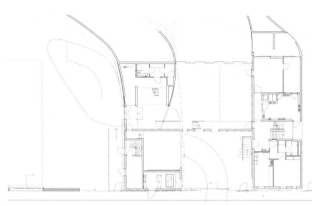

Ground-Floor Plan of Residence

The chancellery, which clearly follows the objectives of the project in terms of image, is presented as a light and translucent construction that allows considerable views of the activities that take place inside the building. The volume that houses the residence, situated closer to the park and conceived as an independent villa integrated into the landscape, adopts a more solid appearance thanks to the stone cladding. A public courtyard was created in between the two structures that provides access to each and allows panoramic views of the surrounding landscape. The gate that surrounds the complex transforms into an external skin that integrates with the building façade, sometimes transparent and at other times closed. The stone-clad volumes were conceived as lodges that connect interior to exterior.

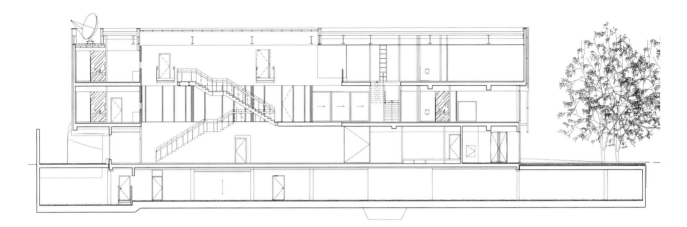

Longitudinal Section of the Chancellery

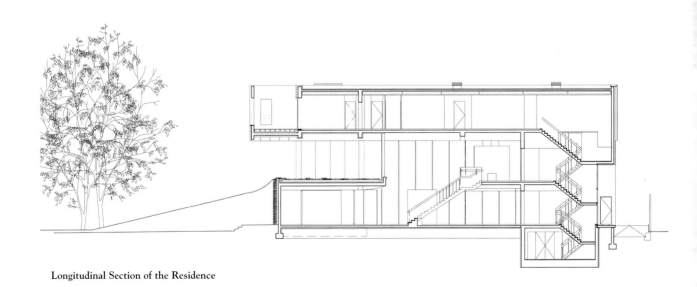

Longitudinal Section of the Residence

The close relationship established by this project with its environment is emphasized by the use of color and texture, coupled with a careful analysis of materials and construction techniques. The façades display a linear and geometric composition derived from the orthogonal layout of the volumes, in contrast to the organic forms of the iron gate, the texture of marble, and the glazed screen. The rationality of the project is reflected in its interior, where spatial relations are potentiated by double-height ceilings, uninterrupted views of the exterior, and visual transparency between both volumes.

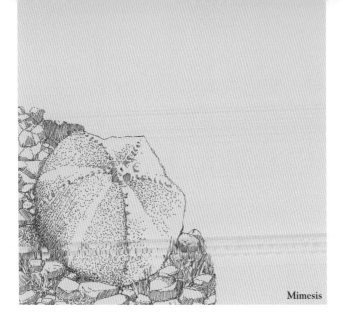

Mimesis

Magasin 3 is a contemporary art gallery, located near Stockholm's old dock area, which over time has incorporated new buildings and outdoor spaces adjacent to the original building to complement the existing services. The program includes a main gallery, an annexed exhibition space, a studio, a café, and a park that today forms part of the city center. The original postwar pavilion is built on a single level and in the traditional vernacular style of Swedish architecture. In 2004, the Block Architecture team received the commission to create an exterior installation in front of the building, with the objective of grouping the different structures that had gradually configured the exhibition complex while lending it a renewed image. The project was to resolve two fundamental issues. First, due to strict planning regulations, the installation had to be as non-intrusive as possible. Second, Magasin 3 would abandon its current headquarters in several years and build a new building to fulfill the needs of the center. After studying the possibilities and exchanging views, the architects agreed on a proposal that adapts to the park environment and at the same time communicates to the visitor that the gallery will soon cease to exist in that place.

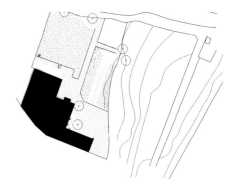

Site Plan

Client
Magasin 3 Gallery

Type of Project
Fence

Location
Stockholm, Sweden

Total Length
217 feet (66 m)

Year of Completion
2004

Photos ©
Graeme Williamson

Magasin 3

Block Architecture

General Plan of Complex

Axonometric View of the Fence

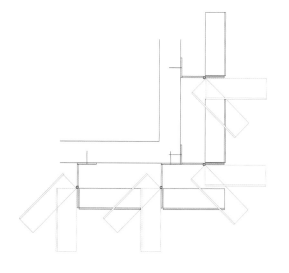

Plan Showing a Construction Detail

The solution consists of a 12-foot (4-m)-high fence that
envelops the complex and adapts to the irregular form of the
general composition from back to front. The fence is comprised of individual wood posts anchored to the terrain and
supported by a structural framework. The posts are coated
by aluminum mirror sheets on one side and fixed to the
structural framework by a series of hinges that allow them
to rotate 270 degrees, as shutters would do. The fence constitutes the new façade of the center, interrupted only by
the access to the gallery. The mirror skin reflects the park
landscape, integrating the constructed element within its
natural context, while the slots in between the planks offer
temporary glimpses of the building and allow it to gradually
disappear.

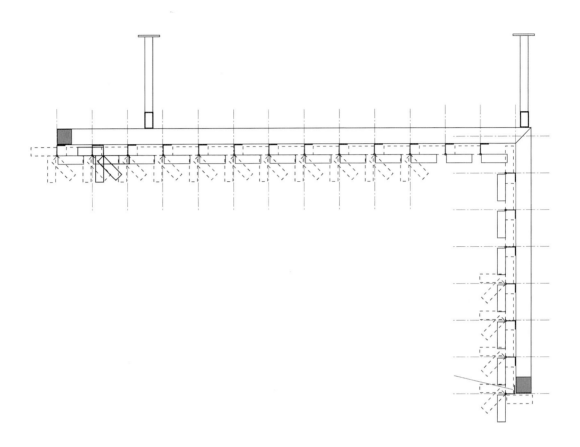

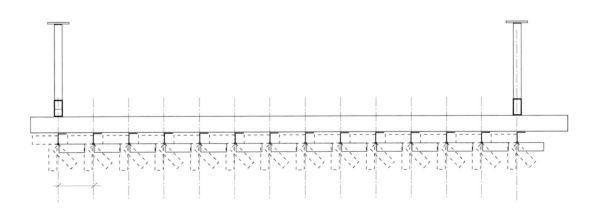

Plans

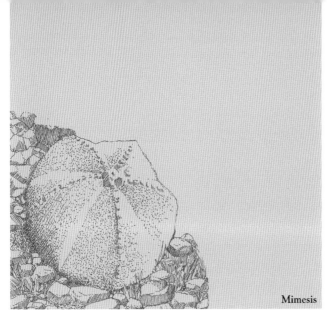

Mimesis

The Risonare Hotel in Kobuchizawa, Japan, is a holiday center specializing in the organization of weddings and other celebrations. Here, hotel guests can find all the spaces and services necessary to celebrate a wedding, including the Leaf Chapel (see p. 164), located within the hotel gardens and designed by the same architects. These ceremonies are a succession of rituals each with its own meaning and designated space specially designed to evoke and enhance the magic of the moment. In this case, the clients wished to expand the infrastructure of services with a new ceremonial space to complement the existing ones. After the Leaf Chapel, built one year before and inspired by a bride's veil, the architects conceived this space thinking of the banquet. In order to integrate the new volume within the lush garden that surrounds the hotel, the architects opted for a radical solution that involved wrapping the small building in slender mirror panels. As a result, the topography, vegetation, and sky are reflected in the building's surface, allowing it to blend into the landscape and creating a glistening effect that captivates and attracts visitors.

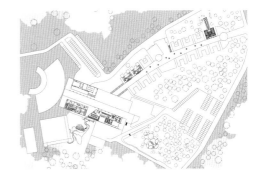

Site Plan

Client
Risonare Hotel

Type of Project
Party pavilion

Location
Kobuchizawa, Japan

Total Surface Area
1,345 square feet (125 m²)

Year of Completion
2005

Photos ©
Daici Ano

Brillare

Klein Dytham Architecture

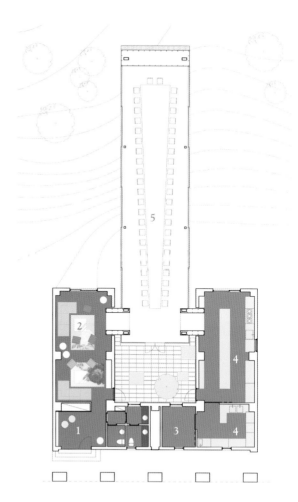

Plan

1- Entrance
2- Reception Room
3- Storage
4- Kitchen
5- Banquet Hall

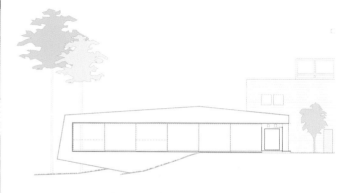

Side Elevation

The main space is a rectangular room with a central table measuring 59 feet (18 m) in length and horizontal windows that look out onto the garden. The trapezoidal form of the table, which seats 22 persons on each side, emphasizes the wider head of the table, intended for the bride and groom. The geometry of the room, together with that of the table, produces the peculiar optical effect of floating in the midst of the encircling forest. White is the dominant color of the room and furniture, except for the delicate botanical drawings that adorn the ceiling. Large sliding windows that run the length of the space complete the integration of the building into the landscape.

Homology (Poplar)   Homology (Elm)   Homology (Ivy)

Homology (Bamboo)   Homology (Pitch Trefoil)   Homology (Oak)

Homologies

The preceding analogies seek to reveal the parallelisms between architecture and plants in which function determines structure. In general, these behaviors or formal adaptations to environmental conditions, in terms of efficiency, allow for the optimal functioning of a living system, or in the case of architecture, an inert one. Functional questions aside, however, and no less interesting with regard to design, are the homologous relations or similarities that can exist between the botanical and the architectural realms. The following analogies, which are purely formal and do not respond to any functional matters, are the result of an exploration of how architecture can imitate or adopt characteristics of the vegetal world solely for aesthetic or evocative purposes. In contemporary architecture, many examples of formal analogies or imitations of plant structures respond to the aim of integrating the concept of nature into the architectural project. This reproduction of vegetal schemes is often the consequence of an intent to integrate the structure within a natural context (to reduce the visual impact of new construction, for example), or to artificially incorporate a natural environment within a highly civilized space as an almost poetic gesture. As a reference for spatial qualities, the vegetal kingdom can lend architecture—particularly that of an organic, sinuous, and apparently chaotic scheme—such typical characteristics of nature as textures, light filters, shadow, and color. This relationship is illustrated by the examples that follow.

Homologies (Pitch Trefoil)

This commission consisted of the creation of a building for the training center and regional offices of Südwestmetall, a metallurgic and electrical company located in the state of Baden-Württemberg, Germany. The site is situated in the central neighborhood of Reutlingen, characterized by its concentration of historical architecture that combines various uses including residences, offices, and small industries. The surrounding urban landscape is defined by low-rise buildings predominantly built in stucco or brick, with wood elements and gabled roofs. The aim of the project is to transmit the company's corporate image while respecting the urban context in which it is located. The scheme consists of three small volumes with inclined roofs that adjust to the scale of existing buildings, and are finished with unusual textures and materials to communicate a new image while preserving traditional forms. A composition based on a botanical pattern extends across the buildings like a carpet, reaching up to 10 feet (3 m) in height. This ornamental and semitransparent element was superimposed on the building's façade and serves to define the boundaries between public and private space, and to generate an open atmosphere in relation to the exterior, resulting in a unique entrance courtyard and city garden.

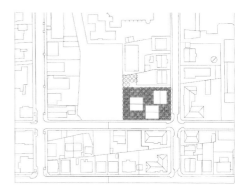

Site Plan

Client
Südwestmetall

Type of Project
Regional offices and training center

Location
Reutlingen, Germany

Total Surface Area
45,208 square feet (4,200 m²)

Year of Completion
2002

Photos ©
Florian Holzherr, Jens Passoth

Südwestmetall Offices

Allmann Sattler Wappner Architekten

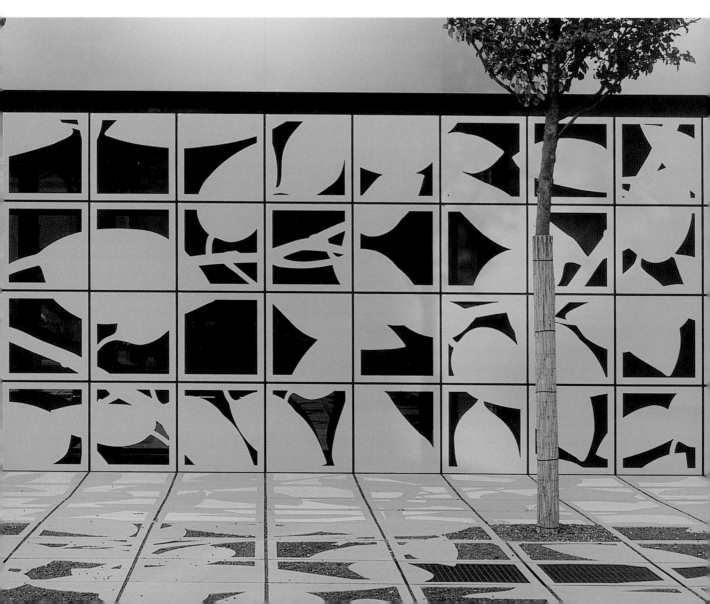

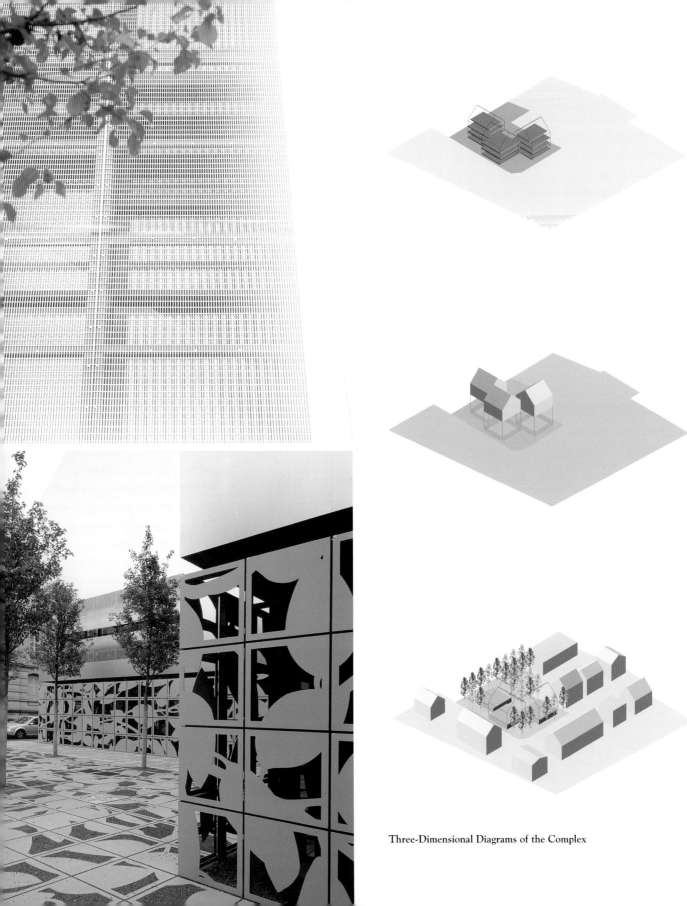

Three-Dimensional Diagrams of the Complex

The singular exterior appearance of the project is lent by a double cladding system used to create the façades. The first layer is mainly composed of full-height insulating glass panels that can be opened individually, while the second consists of 3/16-inch (4-mm) stainless-steel panels fixed onto steel frames. These frames are anchored to the building structure and concealed behind the panels, which are seamlessly joined to emphasize the idea of a continuous skin that envelops the building. The reflective character of the metallic covering transforms the façade into an ever-changing surface that reacts to the tonalities of the different seasons or the changing light throughout the day.

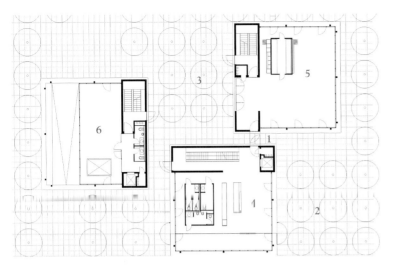

Ground-Floor Plan

1 Public Entrance
2- Public Garden
3- Private Garden
4- Reception Area
5- Cafeteria
6- Private Entrance

Second-Floor Plan

7- Offices
8- Meeting Rooms

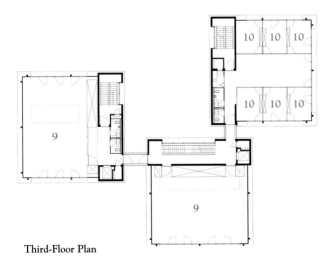

Third-Floor Plan

9- Multipurpose Rooms
10- Offices

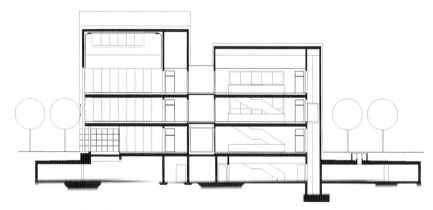

Longitudinal Section

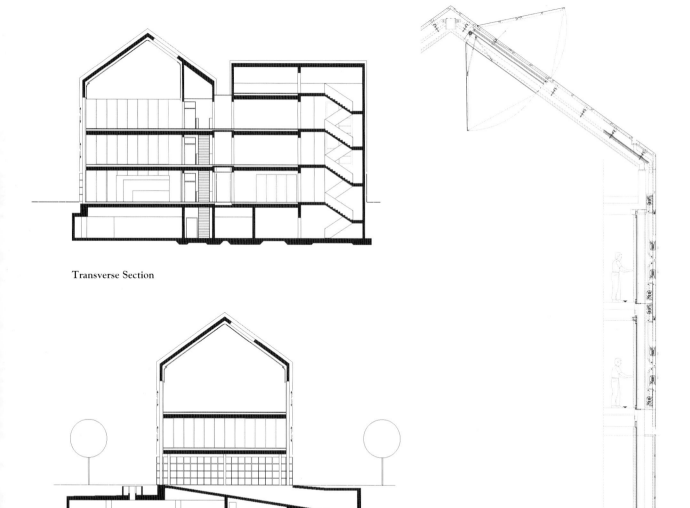

Transverse Section

Transverse Section

Façade Detail

The customer service areas are located on the ground floor as are the entrance, reception area, cafeteria, and access ramps to the parking area. The architects avoided the use of columns and partitions in this area with the intention of creating a sense of openness and a close relationship with the exterior through the perforated steel sheets. The plant forms of the panels create a visual effect similar to that of a garden, replaced by the treetops on the upper levels of the building. Stainless-steel automated shutters control the entry of light. The composition of 3,164 ornamental plates that cover the exterior spaces and base of the building transform it into a sculptural object that seemingly emerges from the site itself.

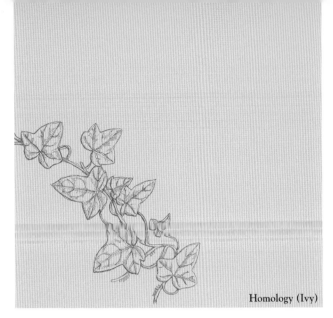

Homology (Ivy)

This singular chapel is situated in the gardens of the Risonare Hotel in Kobuchizawa, a tranquil town in the center of Japan with splendid panoramic views of the most emblematic mountains of the region, such as Mount Fuji and the Yatsugatake peaks. The design for this chapel, mainly destined for wedding celebrations at the hotel, makes the most of the subtle environment and turns the event into a genuinely spectacular experience. Inspired by the forms found in the natural landscape that surrounds the garden, the building is comprised of two leaf-shaped shells—one in glass and the other in steel—that seem to emerge from the ground. The glass leaf displays a delicate pattern and acts as a pergola, which is sustained by a structure similar to the tapered nervation of a leaf. The translucent glass diffuses light to create a more intimate atmosphere in its interior. The white steel leaf is perforated with 4,700 small holes, each of which contains an acrylic lens that filters light and creates a visual effect similar to that of a bride's veil and which changes throughout the day depending on the incidence of light.

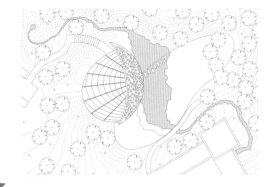

Site Plan

Client
Risonare Hotel

Type of Project
Chapel

Location
Kobuchizawa, Japan

Total Surface Area
2,153 square feet (200 m²)

Year of Completion
2004

Photos ©
Katsuhisa Kida

Leaf Chapel

Preliminary Sketches

Toward the end of the ceremony, when the bride lifts her veil for the traditional kiss, the steel "veil" magically rises in unison to reveal the pond that encircles the chapel and garden. Despite its 11 tons (9,979 kg) in weight, the cylindrical mechanism allows the structure to rise silently, as if it were a weightless piece of fabric, in 38 seconds. In contrast to the dazzling white of the exterior, dark materials and tones were used for the interior in order to emphasize the solemnity of the occasion. The interior is comprised of dark wood walls, wooden pews, black acrylic trellises, and natural granite floors.

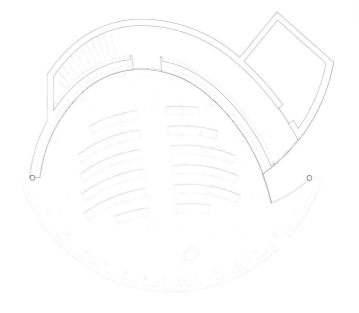

Plan

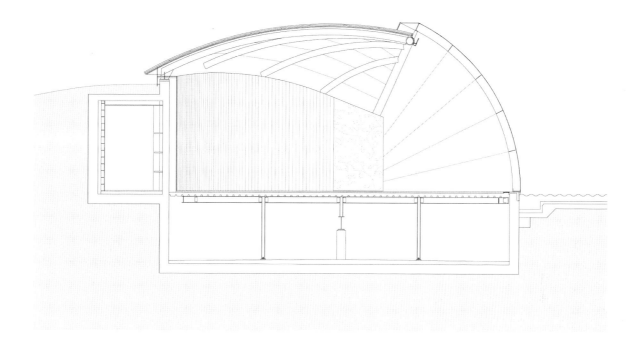

Transverse Section

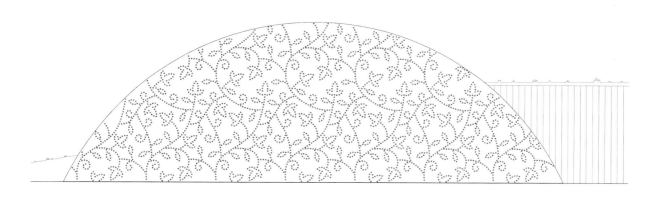

Side Elevation

General Section of the Garden

A wedding under the moonlight can also result in a very dramatic event, thanks to the lace-like effect produced by the perforations of the steel structure at night. The lenses that during the day multiply the effects of natural light turn at night into tiny lanterns that envelop the building and transform it into a sculptural object. The chapel subtly illuminates the garden during the reception after the ceremony. The composition of orifices is inspired by the *rempukusou*, a small yellow flower that grows in the surrounding garden, and the Chinese characters of its name signify good luck and a happy wedding.

Homology (Poplar)

In France, the construction of schools for children in the form of treehouses is not particularly one of the main objectives of the Ministry of Education. Nonetheless, architects Edouard François and Duncan Lewis turned an idea conceived by children into a reality by building a school amidst the treetops. This project began with an old primary school located in Thiais—today a suburb south of Paris—whose classrooms and installations were integrated into the surrounding landscape. Due to an increase in the population of the area, the existing infrastructure of the school could not meet the needs of the growing number of students and required a general renovation of its facilities. The architects took advantage of this restructuring to better organize the campus and give it compositional coherence. The addition was planned with the original master plan of the school in mind, positioned parallel to the existing classroom buildings, with the exception of being entirely suspended and raised 9 feet (3m) from the ground. This scheme situates the new classrooms in a privileged place that enjoys views of the neighboring park and makes use of the space underneath as a play area integrated into the school patio.

Transverse Section

Client
Buffon School

Type of Project
Elementary school addition

Location
Thiais, France

Total Surface Area
3,229 square feet (300 m²)

Year of Completion
2005

Photos ©
Edouard François

Buffon School

Edouard François, Duncan Lewis

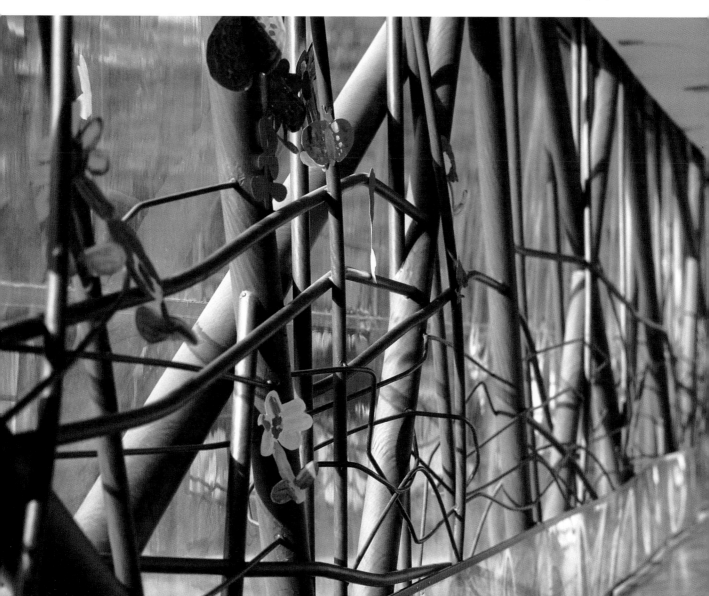

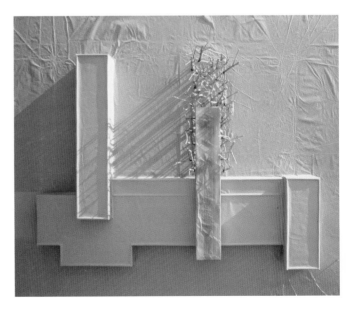

Preliminary Models

The originality of the project lies not only in the structural effort required to elevate the entire block from the ground, but also in the insertion of the volume between two rows of trees that provide structural support. The rectangular volume consists of a steel framework comprised of slender plates situated along the horizontal façades. The safety railing that wraps around the glass façade evokes a composition of vegetal forms that conceal the structure and allow it to blend in with the natural forms of the surrounding trees. Through this project, François and Lewis achieved a veritable fusion of nature and architecture that is manifested in the façade and in the finest of details and interior finishings.

Homology (Bamboo)

The city of Tokyo is packed with tiny buildings inserted into awkward plots that in other cities of the world would most likely end up as residual spaces, but which the Japanese take advantage of to create singular constructions. This characteristic typology of the megalopolis, which architect Yoshiharu Tsukamoto has dubbed "pet architecture," is a result of the continuous divisions of the city due to historical events, current planning policies, and privatized urban initiatives. This project is an example of Klein Dytham Architecture's particular take on pet architecture. The form and size of the building respond to the morphology of the site itself and the maximum size permitted by building regulations. The narrow, two-story volume reaches 36 feet (11 m) in length and has a width of 8 feet (2.5 m) on one side and 24 inches (60 cm) on the opposite side. Despite its reduced dimensions, the building occupies a prominent place within the urban context, as its wider façade looks onto a busy commercial street. This not only attracts the attention of passers-by, but also provides the interior spaces with natural light and ventilation. Given the characteristics of the volume and the client's request for a multifunctional commercial space, the project was conceived as a large inhabitable billboard.

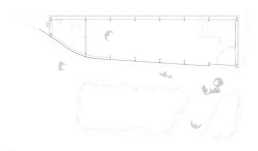

Site Plan

Client
Risa Partners

Type of Project
Commercial space

Location
Tokyo, Japan

Total Surface Area
1,808 square feet (168 m²)

Year of Completion
2005

Photos ©
Daici Ano

Billboard Building

Klein Dytham Architecture

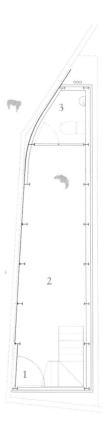

Ground-Floor Plan

1- Entrance
2- Retail
3- Service

Second-Floor Plan

4- Office
5- Storage

The most important element of the project is the 36-foot (11-m) façade, whose image embodies the character of the building. Due to the narrow proportions of the volume, the architects preferred to distract attention from the construction itself by playing with images and transparencies to generate the illusion of a plantation of trees, as if the project entailed the creation of an urban garden rather than a building. The silhouette of a simple image of bamboo was applied to the glass of the main façade, while the back wall inside the space was painted green. During the day, the silhouettes filter the light into the interior space, and at night the green light that shines from within creates the effect of a small plantation in the midst of the city.

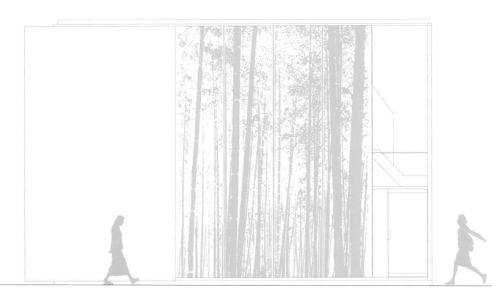

Elevation

Homology (Bamboo)

The Cisneros Fontanals Art Foundation is a nonprofit organization established in 2002 to support cultural exchange within the visual arts. The founder, Ella Fontanals, originally from Venezuela and based in Miami, decided with her family to create this organization for the promotion of emerging and multidisciplinary contemporary artists from Latin America. The center was to house offices, studios, and a large exhibition area flexible enough to host a busy program throughout the year. The industrial character of the chosen location for the building determined the primary guideline for the project: to humanize this area of the city dominated by a landscape of industrial warehouses. The decision to create an urban garden that would not only provide the building with a distinctive appearance, but also serve to lend a more pleasant atmosphere to the area, was realized by applying an image of a bamboo forest onto the façades of the building. The public spaces surrounding the center were planted with real bamboo to emphasize the idea of an urban garden. Not surprisingly, the project has become an iconic component of this neighborhood thanks to this powerful and singular image within the urban context.

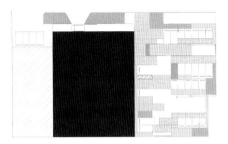

Site Plan

Client
Cisneros Fontanals Art Foundation

Type of Project
Cultural center

Location
Miami, Florida

Total Surface Area
35,521 square feet (3,300 m^2)

Year of Completion
2006

Photos ©
Daniel Romero, Walter Robinson, Oriol Tarridas, Mónica Vázquez

Miami, Florida

Cisneros Fontanals Art Foundation

René González

Photomontage

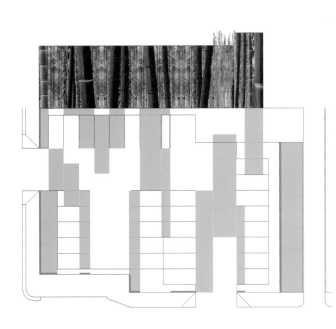

Photomontage of Elevation and Plan

The general composition of plant patterns was achieved through the application of colored-glass mosaic tiles that are arranged together like pixels to generate an image. The parking area in front of the main access incorporates different tones of green to reinforce the idea of an urban garden. As the visitor approaches the building, the perception of the jungle at a distance gradually dissolves into random organic patterns and colors. The colorful and organic scheme offers an alternative to the traditional image of art centers characterized by simple materials, neutral forms, and white backgrounds, and also fosters an active exchange between the city and the artistic community.

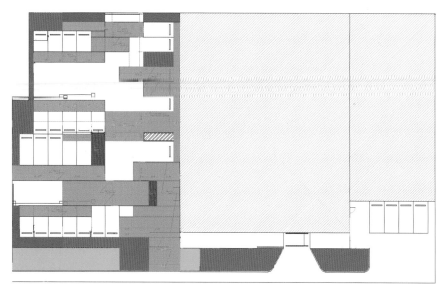

Exterior Plan

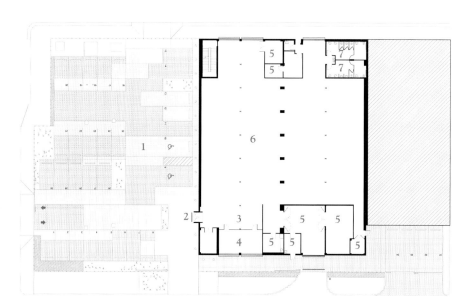

Ground-Floor Plan

1- Parking
2- Entrance
3- Reception Area
4- Conference Room
5- Storage
6- Exhibition Area
7- Services

Index of Architects

Allmann Sattler Wappner Architekten
125 Nymphenburger Strasse, Munich 80636, Germany
T: +49 (0)89 13 99 25 0
F: +49 (0)89 13 99 25 99
info@allmannsattlerwappner.de
www.allmannsattlerwappner.de

Alsop Architects
Parkgate Studio, 41 Parkgate Road, London SW11 4NP, United Kingdom
T: +44 (0)20 7978 7878
F: +44 (0)20 7978 7879
www.alsoparchitects.com

Auer + Weber + Assoziierte
Georgenstrasse 22, Munich 80799, Germany
T: +49 (0)89 381 617 0
F: +49 (0)89 381 617 38
muenchen@auer-weber.de
www.auer-weber.de

Atelier Tekuto
301, 6-15-16 Honkomagome, Bonkyo-ku, Tokyo 113-0021, Japan
T: +81 3 5940 2770
F: +81 3 5940 2780
info@tekuto.com
www.tekuto.com

Block Architecture
83a Geffrye Street, London E2 8HX, United Kingdom
T: +44 (0)20 7729 9193
F: +44 (0)20 7729 9193
mail@blockarchitecture.com
www.blockarchitecture.com

Claesson Koivisto Rune
Sankt Paulsgatan 25, Stockholm 118-48, Sweden
T: +46 8 644 5863
F: +46 8 644 5883
arkitektkontor@claesson-koivisto-rune.se
www.claesson-koivisto-rune.se

Edouard François
136 Rue Falguière, Paris 75015, France
T: +33 1 45 67 88 87
F: +33 1 45 67 51 45
agence@edouardfrancoise.com
www.edouardfrancoise.com

Erick van Egeraat Associated Architects
Calandstraat 23, Rotterdam 3016 CA, Netherlands
T: +31 (0)10 436 9686
F: +31 (0)10 436 9573
eea.nl@eea-architects.com
www.eea-architects.com

Eskew + Dumez + Ripple
365 Canal Street, Suite 3150, New Orleans, LA 70130, United States
T: +1 504 561 8686
www.studioedr.com

Factor Architecten
Geograaf 40, Duiven 6921 EW, Netherlands
T: +31 (0)26 38 44 460
F: +31 (0)26 38 44479
info@factorarchitecten.nl
www.factorarchitecten.nl

Jarmund/Vigsnæs Architects
Hausmannsgate 6, Oslo 0186, Norway
T: +47 22 99 4343
F: +47 22 99 4353
jva@jva.no
www.jva.no

Klein Dytham Architecture
Deluxe, 1-3-3 Azabu Juban, Minato-ku, Tokyo 106-0045, Japan
T: +81 3 3505-5347
kda@klein-dytham.com
www.klein-dytham.com

Korteknie Stuhlmacher Architecten
Postbus 25012, Rotterdam 2001 HA, Netherlands
T: +31 (0)10 425 94 41
F: +31 (0)10 466 51 55
www.kortekniestuhlmacher.nl

Laboratory of Architecture
General Francisco Ramírez 5B, Col. Ampliación Daniel Garza 11840,
Mexico
T: +52 (55) 2614 1060, ext. 109
www.laboratoryofarchitecture.com

Lake | Flato Architects
311 3rd Street, Suite 200, San Antonio, TX 78205, United States
T: +1 210 227 3335
F: +1 210 224 9515
www.lakeflato.com

Masahiro Ikeda
201 Silhouette-Ohyamacho 1-20, Ohyama-cho, Shibuya, Tokyo 151-0065,
Japan
T: +81 3 5738 5564
F: +81 3 5738 5565
info@miascoltd.net
www.miascoltd.net

Miha Kajzelj
Bratov Uāakar 66, Ljubljana 1000, Slovenia
T: +38 6 4151 9086
F: +38 6 1423 4446

Pugh + Scarpa
225 Michigan Ave. F1, Santa Monica, CA 90404, United States
T: +1 310 828 0226
www.pugh-scarpa.com

Rene Gonzalez
5582-4 Northeast 4 Court, Miami, FL 33137, United States
T: +1 305 762 5895
F: +1 305 762 5896
www.renegonzalezarchitect.com

Roldán + Berengué Arquitectos
Albareda 12 Bajos, Local B, Barcelona 08004, Spain
T: +34 93 441 4399
F: +34 93 324 8085
roldan&berengue@coac.net

Sauerbruch Hutton Architects
Lehrter Strasse 57, Berlin 10557, Germany
T: +49 30 397 821 20
F: +49 30 397 821 30
pr@sauerbruchhutton.de
www.sauerbruchhutton.de

Studio Pali Fekete Architects
8609 E. Washington Blvd., Culver City, CA 90232, United States
T: +1 310 558 0902
F: +1 310 558 0904
www.spfa.com

Steven Holl Architects
450 W 31st Street, 11th Floor, New York, NY 10001, United States
T: +1 212 629 7262
F: +1 212 629 7312
mail@stevenholl.com
www.stevenholl.com